THE
GLASGOW NAVY
The ships of the Clyde Navigation Trust

Part One: The *CLUTHAS*

Brian Patton

ISBN 978-0-9564288-3-7

First published in Scotland in 2013 by Brian Patton

Printed and bound by
Martins the Printers Limited
Seaview Works, Spittal
Berwick-upon-Tweed, TD15 1RS
www.martins-the-printers.com

Design by www.simprimstudio.com
Set in Frutiger and Minion Pro

Contents

A view of the Clyde at Clyde Street ferry, with one *CLUTHA* making her way down river, while a second, one of the first four steamers, pulls out from Springfield Lane landing. Several Laird Line ships lie at Lancefield Quay and there are some sailing ships in the distance. This is a commercial postcard, but as it was not sent until October 1948, the postmark is of no help in dating it. (*Author's collection*)

Introduction

One feature of Glasgow's public transport which is almost forgotten to-day is the Clutha service, which from 1884 to 1903 provided a cheap and frequent service of steamers up and down the Clyde between Victoria Bridge at Stockwell Street and Whiteinch. These vessels, which began running in the spring of 1884, soon found favour with the public and annual patronage grew to over three million passengers. Then first the Subway opened, then electric trams began to operate on the city's streets and patronage of the little steamers declined sharply. They faded out of existence on a miserable November night in 1903, with little notice being taken of their departure from the scene and to-day no one can remember them. Unlike the history of the trams and, to a lesser extent the Subway, little has been written about the *Cluthas*. Strangely, Messrs Duckworth and Langmuir, who so ably chronicled the shipping in the west of Scotland, did not cover their story, making only a brief reference to a short section in one of Andrew McQueen's books on Clyde steamers and the only other published account is an article on the work of the Clyde Navigation Trust, which appeared in *The Engineer* in 1888. It seemed that it was time for a more detailed history.

The harbour of Glasgow was originally managed by what was then the Town Council, but as trade developed with the deepening of the Clyde in the late 18th century, this arrangement was no longer satisfactory and in 1809 the River Improvement Trust was set up to oversee the harbour. It was enlarged by Act of Parliament in 1840 when among other changes, it was given powers "to establish and operate boats for the convenience of persons crossing from one side of the Harbour to the other". In due course ferries, worked by rowing boats, were opened at York Street and Clyde Street and the old-established horse and passenger ferry at Govan was acquired by the Trust in 1857.

As the port continued to develop, the Improvement Trust was considered to be no longer adequate for the task of managing it and in 1858 it was, by Act of Parliament, replaced by the Trustees of the Clyde Navigation, a body with a wider membership and greater powers. The outer limit of the harbour was set at the mouth of the River Kelvin. There was always a certain amount of common membership of the Trust and the Town Council/City Corporation, mostly drawn from the relatively small business world of the city, and of course Trust members would frequently meet those from other bodies and commercial firms in places such as the Stock Exchange, the Chamber of Commerce and private clubs.

The Clutha service run by the Clyde Navigation Trust was authorised by Act of Parliament of 1878 and came under the remit of its Ferries Committee, which met about eight times each year. However, other committees and individuals had fingers in this particular pie. The Works Committee (sometimes called the New Works Committee) was responsible for such items as landing places, the General Manager had a say in daily operations, the Engineer had a good deal to do with the service and the Law Committee dealt with any claims arising from accidents. There was also the Management Committee, which was in fact the full Trust sitting in committee. It should in passing be mentioned that for much of the period when the *CLUTHAS* were in service, there was no General Manager in post and perhaps their story might have been different had there been, since it sometimes seems that, in the 1890s, no one had an overall picture of what was happening within the Trust, let alone in the wider field of the city's transport.

There was no set budget for the Clutha service, nor indeed for the ferries and accounting and budgetary control, in any modern sense, did not exist within the Trust until a decade after the *CLUTHAS* departed from the river. As long as revenue exceeded running costs, there was no problem for the Trust as a whole and out-of-course expenditure could be met from general Trust finance. A result of this piecemeal approach was that decision-making was slow and sometimes convoluted and different accounts are given by different sources. The detail recorded in minutes and reports also varies considerably over the years, suggesting a sometimes muddled process and, for the historian, it has not always been easy to piece together the whole story. Even in such straightforward matters as annual revenue and passenger numbers different figures are given in different sources; the figures used by Mr Young in his report of 1902 do not tally exactly with those given by Mr McKechnie in his earlier report, although the trend is the same in both documents.

With all the reservations outlined above, this is the story of a part of what was often called "The Glasgow Navy".

Acknowledgement
It would not have been possible to compile this account without the unstinting help given by the staff of the Mitchell Library and I would like to record my warmest thanks to Dr I O'Brien and all the team of the Archives, to Mrs P Grant and the staff of the Glasgow Room and to the photographers.

Brian Patton
Foulden, Berwickshire
9 July 2013

01 The Origins of the Service

As Glasgow harbour developed, housing for those working in it spread along the river banks and many shipyards were established. Old paths along the banks were closed off and the demand for transport along the river grew. Horse buses and later horse trams (north side) and steam trams (south side) provided a service on the roads parallel to the river, but, especially on the north bank these lay at some distance inland and the trams were not very convenient for those living and working near the river. The question of establishing a service of "up and down" steamers on the river (as opposed to the cross-river ferries) seems to have been first considered by the Clyde Navigation Trust at some point in 1877 and on 12 October of that year members of the Ferries Committee sailed on one of the Trust's harbour ferries from Glasgow Bridge to Whiteinch, against a strong wind. Their conclusion was that such a venture seemed promising but it would be necessary to use more powerful boats and the matter was deferred for further consideration. However, it was agreed on 24 October that it would be desirable, in the Bill which was to be presented to Parliament in 1878, to request powers to establish the service, to be worked either by the Trust or by "neutral parties" and this was duly done. The powers granted by section 9 of the Act of 1878 allowed the Trust to run a service "for the conveyance of passengers from and to any place within the limits of the Harbour and adjacent thereto". The Trust could either work the service itself or by agreement with any person or company willing to provide, maintain and work it. The maximum fare authorised was 2d.

At its meeting of 6 August of that year, on a motion of George Browne, the consideration of establishing this service was remitted to the Ferries Committee. It was discussed at the meeting of 8 October, which Mr Thomas Seath, shipbuilder of Rutherglen, attended, to give members details of the vessels with which he had formerly maintained a successful service between that town and the city, though he was careful to point out that that service had run only in summertime. He considered that the boats used should be twin-screw vessels, about 70ft (21.62m) in length and 12ft (3.65m) in beam and be capable of attaining 10mph (16km/hr). These would cost about £1,650 each. The crew should consist of three men or two men and a boy. The existing ferry stairs would make suitable calling points. Mr Seath stressed that he had no interest in running the service himself. No decision was taken on the matter, but Mr. Seath submitted drawings of the proposed ships to the next meeting of the Committee, held on 7 November. These were now to be of the length earlier suggested but 15ft (4.60m) wide. He was then asked to submit detailed plans. These would seem not to have been forthcoming and nothing further happened until the meeting of the Trust on 30 August 1879 when Mr Browne, who was perhaps impatient with the lack of progress, gave notice of a motion to start such a service, which he would introduce to the following meeting on 10 October. This motion was defeated on grounds of expense and the matter was again deferred. Nothing daunted, the Ferries Committee on 17 November resolved to ask the Trust's Engineer, Mr James Deas, to report on the ferry landings and other places which might be required for the service. An offer from a Mr Peter Denniston to run the service was considered but his proposal was declined. During the next two years, nothing further was done about the proposal, although the report by the Engineer was received on 8 May 1880.

In this report, Mr Deas said "The only economical way I can see for Landing Places for these steamers is for them to be constructed at bow and stern (so) as to use the present Ferry Stairs". Evidently this had also been the plan of Mr Denniston. Clearly to work easily, the boats would have to be double-ended. Mr Deas went on to add that he *could* design a landing stage of a simple form if necessary but he urged committee members to consider the amount of quay space and shed accommodation which might be lost if such stages were constructed. He estimated this to be, for each stage, anything between 73 and 100 feet (22.25m and 30.43m) in length. The pontoons forming these stages would be linked to the bank by a gangway 90 feet (27.43m) in length and, with disabled or infirm passengers in mind (an unusual consideration for the time), he recommended that the gradient should be not more than 1 in 7. He also reminded members that an omnibus service which had been serving Queen's Dock from the city by a route along the north bank had been withdrawn due to lack of patronage. He envisaged landing places at the two city termini of Victoria Bridge and Glasgow (Jamaica) Bridge, at neither of which there were ferry stairs, York Street (north and south), Clyde Street (north and south), Finnieston (north and south), Highland Lane (on the south bank) and Queen's Dock.

Based on this report, the Ferries Committee decided on 15 February 1881 to obtain a set of plans for the design of a boat suitable for using the existing ferry stairs as a landing place. These were submitted by Mr Deas on 14 June, but the Committee decided to defer further consideration of the matter, as it would be "premature" to establish such a service. Mr J L Mitchell, who was now the main driving force behind the plans, dissented from this view, but as no other member supported him, the question was left in abeyance. At the meeting of the full Trust on 29 July, consideration of the matter was likewise deferred and Mr Browne, at the request of Mr Mitchell (who could not be present), gave notice that the latter would present an amendment to the next meeting, which took place on 16 August. He duly did so and it was now decided to refer the whole question to a special joint committee of the Ferries and Harbour Committees and, if they agreed to go ahead with the plan, to consider whether the service should be run by the Trust itself or by parties willing to undertake it. The special committee should also be empowered to take advice with regard to floating landing stages. The Trust agreed to this proposal, with the addition of members of the New Works Committee to the special committee.

The special joint committee met on 18 October and authorised Messrs Browne, Dunn and Mitchell to confer with a consultant, one Mr Strain, on the question of landing stages, without in any way committing themselves to anything. Mr. Strain presented his report on 12 January 1882 (T.CN-3.303). He suggested doing away with the stairs and in their recesses installing a kind of pontoon, to be used by both the ferries and the new steamers. He stressed that the service should be frequent, that the boats should be swift and easily manoeuvred and that landing places should not project into the river. Mr Mitchell read this and, having had a meeting with Mr. Strain, asked Mr Deas to consider these proposals and obtain an estimate of cost. This resulted in another report dated 1 September 1882, written by a Mr David Weddell, who recommended that designs and estimates for boats to use the ferry landings should be obtained by the Engineer. He considered Mr Strain's plan "objectionable", as it could cost up to £7,000 to construct a pair of recesses of the kind envisaged. On 19 December, Mr Mitchell suggested that the Trust should construct two ferry boats, of the existing type, and with these start a service between Victoria Bridge and Pointhouse. If the service proved to be unsuccessful, the boats could then be used on cross-river ferry services. Those present were evenly divided on the question and the proposal was carried by the convener's vote.

Meanwhile, early in 1883, the Trust had received memorials (memorandums) from shipowners and residents of Govan and district, supporting the idea of a service on the river. These were on 15 March referred to the Committee of Management which, on a motion of Mr Mitchell, set up a new, slimmer sub-committee to consider the question further. This sub-committee consisted of Messrs Browne, Mitchell, Smith and Renny Watson. Mr Mitchell, who chaired it and wrote its report (T.CN 3-325), was particularly enthusiastic, although at times it would seem that his enthusiasm got the better of his business sense. The report, which at first outlined a service starting at Albert Bridge, was favourable to the idea, basing an estimate of its likely success on the premise that about fourteen and a half million passengers per year then used the cross-river ferries and the trams which ran between Glasgow and Govan and Glasgow and Partick/Whiteinch. The Vale of Clyde Tramways Company, running from Govan to Paisley Road Toll, carried three and a half million passengers in 1882, its best year, and if even a small number of these took to the new service, it would be profitable. It was considered that the ferries might lose about 5% of their traffic and the financial consequences of this were offset against the profit which the steamers would make. The projected annual account, which did not include any figure for repairs, was as follows:-

Cost per day of running a service with three boats in operation:-

Interest on cost of three boats at £1,500 each	£1/13/-
Wages of three men	£2/16/-
Coal for 42 hours steaming	£1/1/-
Oil, waste etc	10/-
Total	£6/-/-
Revenue per day from 2,520 passengers at 1d each	£10/10/-
Less loss of ferry revenue	£2/7/11d
Daily profit	£2/2/1d

The idea of serving Albert Bridge had to be abandoned, due to problems of dredging the stretch of water between that point and Victoria Bridge. Three boats would provide a 15 minute service between the latter and Govan. (T.CN 3 325)

In November 1883 Mr Mitchell became Convener of the Ferries Committee.

On the basis of this somewhat slender evidence and a good deal of optimism, the Trust decided to go ahead with the proposal. The matter was then passed to the Ferries Committee to progress. Drawings of the steamers were presented by a Mr White and once again by Mr Seath and it was to be his design which was preferred. The steamers were to be single-ended. The dimensions were fixed at 70ft (21.33m) x 13ft (3.95m) and the vessels were to be propelled by twin screws and have a capacity of 250 passengers. It was agreed on 20 March that two were to be ordered from T.B. Seath and Co. at £2,050 each, this total being very soon (on 3 April) increased to four, at £2,000 each, thus increasing the cost by 77% over Mr Mitchell's estimate. It was confirmed that ferry stairs would be used as landings. It was reported on 26 December that good progress was being made on the boats. On 2 January 1884 Messrs Dunn and McOnie were asked to report on landing places above Glasgow Bridge and at Whiteinch and Partick, where there were no ferry stairs, and they suggested on 11 January 1884 that there should be punts, protected by piles, at Glasgow

Bridge and stairs at Victoria Bridge, where a waiting room and space for coal and stores were to be provided. The western terminus of the service was to be at Sawmill Road. At the same meeting, "Clutha", the Latin name for the river, was agreed for the steamers, although it was not recorded who suggested it. In practice, at least in earlier years, the boats were generally referred to by the Trust as "harbour steamers" or "up and down steamers". The vessels were named *CLUTHA No.1* to *CLUTHA No.4* and did not carry any other name. The first was launched on 14 January and was named by the daughter of one of the Trustees. Crews were appointed in March and the Ferries Committee decided that the after cabin was to be reserved for ladies, on payment of a supplementary fare of 1d. There is no record that this proposal was put into practice. At some point it was decided that there should be a crew of four on each vessel, the additional member being a young lad. As these would be paid between 2/6d and 3/3d per day, the original estimate of the wages bill had to be increased by between 10/- and 13/- per day.

A formal inauguration took place in bright weather on 11 April, when *No.1* and *No.2* conveyed members of the Trust and other local dignitaries on a cruise to Bowling. Lunch was served on board, from tables complete with white tablecloths, laid out in each saloon; it must have been a cold repast as there were no facilities for heating food on board. The tables and, presumably, chairs, were installed for the day and were not part of the usual furniture. Public service began on the following day and the new facility was well received, takings during the first week being £120/16/5, with £103/13/11 in the following week. The latter figure would suggest loadings in the region of 24,000 per week, allowing for those who travelled free. During May 101,920 passengers were carried, with receipts of £424/13/4d. A census of each landing was taken on Thursday 24 June, a day of showery weather, and it showed the following pattern of usage:-

7.00am to 8.40am	274 passengers
9.00am to 3.40pm	1,425 passengers
4.10 to 6.10pm	632 passengers
Evening	491 passengers
Total	2,822 passengers

On that day, 1,083 passengers disembarked and 1,254 boarded at the two city stages. These figures set the pattern for carryings for the rest of the time of the *CLUTHAS*, with the later addition of workmen's boats in the early morning. As the service had not yet been extended to Whiteinch, Sawmill Road was quite busy, handling 653 passengers. It seemed that Mr Mitchell and his committee had in fact under-estimated the demand for the river service, although they had also under-estimated the costs. The success of the venture led to the ordering of two additional boats (*No.5* and *No.6*) from Mr Seath on 13 June. They were to be 30ft (9.14m) longer and 1ft (0.30m) wider than the first four and be capable of a speed of 12mph (19.30km/hr). Nothing was said about their being suitable for ferry stairs. The first of these entered service early in August and proved to be satisfactory.

It would seem, from an article in *The Bailie*, that Mr Mitchell was not averse to taking credit for the entire scheme and he had certainly done much to bring about the execution of the plans, often in the face of official prevarication. Without his enthusiasm and drive, the service might not have come into existence. However, these plans, in a rudimentary form at least, had been discussed since 1878, two years before he had even become a member of the Trust and not all the glory was rightfully his.

02 Operating the *CLUTHAS* – early days

The original pattern of service, starting from Victoria Bridge, offered calls at Glasgow Bridge, Clyde Street ferry (north and south), Finnieston (north and south), Kelvinhaugh (north), Highland Lane (south side), Partick Wharf (Pointhouse), Water Row (Govan) Meadowside and Sawmill Road.

It soon became apparent that there were several problems with the service and the steamers, requiring action by the Ferries Committee. The calls at Finnieston south side must have been either difficult or unremunerative, since as early as 15 April there was a discussion about abandoning these and they were discontinued from 13 May. It was also decided on 13 May to employ a Superintendent for the service and a Mr Scott was duly appointed. He was clearly not successful in the post, since he was dismissed on 20 January 1885, without immediate replacement. There had been comments from passengers about the two sewers which discharged into the river beside the landings at Glasgow and Victoria Bridges and on 28 April the Clerk to the Police was asked to divert these. He replied that it was not possible to do so and instead proposed to cover the outlets. Even so, the atmosphere must have been distinctly unsalubrious at times for waiting passengers.

Although not specifically mentioned in the minutes, the matter of the use of the ferry stairs by the steamers must have been uppermost in the minds of the members of the Ferries Committee when they met on 10 July 1884. It was agreed without any objections to discontinue calls at Clyde Street (both north and south) and Kelvinhaugh (north side), as passenger numbers were low at these points, and the question of constructing a landing stage at Kelvinhaugh south side (Highland Lane) was discussed. The General Manager and Engineer had been asked to consider new arrangements for Govan and Pointhouse and these were approved on 10 August. At Govan, steamers were being detained by the vehicle ferry and it was decided that they should instead call at the adjacent stairs, with additional piling being fitted. A ramp should be constructed at Pointhouse to obviate the need for boats to enter the Kelvin. The stairs at the two city termini should be enclosed with fencing. The proposed ramp at Pointhouse was not constructed, as on 14 August it was agreed that steamers should instead call at the north side vehicle ferry slip. On 25 August it was decided to provide a floating stage at Highland Lane. On board the steamers, the steering position should be railed off, as the man at the helm could scarcely concentrate on steering the steamer when jostled by passengers. There should be more seats on deck and the height of the funnels should be increased. In June it was reported that Mr Seath was altering the boats to take account of these points. In the same month, an offer received from a Mr William Burns, to provide a refreshment service on board the steamers, was declined by the Ferries Committee. Additional crews should be recruited, as there were complaints about the necessity for men to work long hours. On 28 April a minor collision between *No.3* and the schooner *LADY HELEN* off Robertson Street brought to light some problems with the machinery; new pins were required and the joints of the boilers were not sufficiently tight. Mr Deas and a Mr Hazelton Robson were then asked to inspect the hulls, boilers and machinery of the steamers, to discuss matters with Mr Seath and to prepare a report. This was received on 10 July but the contents were kept confidential and it can only be supposed that remedial measures were being put in place. There had been some accidents to passengers and on 15 April a child was seriously injured at Kelvinhaugh when disembarking from *No.2*. The matter was settled for the not-inconsiderable sum of £50 (about £10,000 in present-day values).Twelve days later an elocution teacher, Mr J Hay was injured when he jumped off *No.3* at Clyde Street south side and fell on the steps. He later claimed £1,000 damages but the Trust refused to pay this amount, making instead an unspecified offer, which was declined. In August *No.1* was hit by the jib of a crane at Custom House Quay, but neither boat nor passengers suffered any injury. Perhaps the funnels were still on the short side, since on 12 March 1885 a Dr Shaw of Govan claimed for damage to his coat by a cinder; the Ferries Committee agreed to pay for the repair.

Strangely, the most serious problem to occur was mentioned only by implication in official records. There had been no trial of the use of ferry stairs by passengers in day-to-day conditions and it very quickly proved to be impracticable. Firstly, there must have been some difficulties in interworking with the intensive service of the ferries. Being single-ended, the *CLUTHAS* had to go astern out into the river when leaving a landing place and that must have taken up some additional time, as well as being a tricky manoeuvre when the river was busy. *No.1-No.4* were more than 23ft (7m) longer than the latest ferry (*No.8* of 1882) and the stern thus projected out into the river while the boat was at the stairs. As the Clyde could then flow at anything up to 150ft (45.72m) per minute in ordinary conditions and up to 500ft (152.4m) per minute in flood, the vessels were often swung round, making it impossible to align the bow with the steps to allow passengers to board or disembark and the service was consequently delayed. After less than three months operation, the talents of Mr Deas had to be called upon to provide the alternative solution outlined in his report of 1880 and he "very expeditiously" produced a design for a floating landing stage. (T. CN 3-337). The question of serving Clyde Street (north and south side), Finnieston (south side) and Kelvinhaugh (north side) had been solved by simply abandoning calls at these points and landing stages or stairs were introduced at other points, as detailed in Ch6. It does seem strange that an engineer of his experience went so badly wrong with his initial recommendations.

Despite all these teething troubles, there could be no doubt about the success of the venture. *No.5* was in service by 10 August and was reported to be working well. The cost of the two additional boats was £2,500 each.

On 15 October it was decided to reduce the frequency of sailings with effect from 3 November. There was now a half-hourly service and passenger numbers fell to 36,999 in December. *No. 5* and *No. 6* were laid up for the winter. With consideration of Glasgow's winter climate, waiting rooms were now provided at Glasgow Bridge, Kelvinhaugh and Govan and oilskins were issued to masters of the steamers. On 22 December it was decided to extend sailings to Whiteinch. The total income for the 37 weeks operated in 1884 was £1,571/1/10d, or an average of about £42.45 per week, a good deal below Mr Mitchell's original estimate. Unfortunately Sawmill Road had proved to be the home of some "idle boys" who used the landing as a playground, especially on Sundays, and it had to be fenced off.

Traffic remained below expectations in the first six months of 1885, during which 193,645 passengers brought in a revenue of £806/19/1d, £31 per week. However, traffic obviously increased when summer came and in the second half of the year, the steamers carried 919,683 passengers. Their future now appeared to be secure.

Nothing had so far been published about costs, but there clearly were some concerns and on 19 August 1885 a sub-committee of the Ferries Committee was set up to consider the financial position. Income to the year ending 30 June 1885 was £4,638/17/6d, but expenditure was £5,855/19/8d, of which wages accounted for £2,061/15/9d, coal £1,284/10/2d and repairs £1804/9/-. This was more than twice the estimates, which did not include any figure for repairs, although Mr. Mitchell could hardly have expected that so much would have to be spent on new steamers and it suggests that there had been many problems. There had been damages to the value of £74/6/7d but in some cases this was recouped from other parties to the accidents concerned. Capital expenditure was given as £775/18/- but it is not clear what was covered by this, or if it was included in the expenses. What was clear was that there had been a deficit of at least £1,217. The sub-committee reported on 27 August, with the regret that "so much expenditure should have been required on additions and improvements to the boats". Word about the problems must have spread around Clydeside, since on 16 March1886 a letter was received from one Mr John Melville, offering to buy *No.5* and *No.6* and he was invited to submit an offer. Nothing further was heard from him. In any case, it was agreed to keep the service going for another year and these boats would be required for it. A decline in receipts for the first six months of 1886 was attributed to the severe weather and to the dullness of trade. It had already been agreed, on 10 February, to increase revenue by allowing advertisements to be placed on the steamers and in the shelters at landing stages and this brought in £76 in the following year. The service between Govan and Whiteinch seems to have catered mainly for leisure traffic in its early days and on 15 October 1886 the Ferries Committee decided that winter sailings should not go beyond Meadowside. (qv Ch5, fares.) In March of the following year they were extended to Whiteinch on Saturdays and at holiday periods and at a later date, probably 1891,Whiteinch became the terminus for all sailings.

In May 1886 someone signing himself "A shipowner and a ratepayer" published a small pamphlet under the title "Our Harbour Boats" which was in effect a diatribe against the *CLUTHAS*. He claimed that the running of the service to Whiteinch and the construction of landing stages at Sawmill Road and Smith Street (Whiteinch) were not covered by the powers granted to the Trust under the Act of 1878 and that they were therefore acting ultra vires, a state of affairs which could lead to prosecution. However, despite the veiled threat, nothing came of this polemic.

The confidence shown in the service was not misplaced, since shortly afterwards revenue began to increase; by January 1888 the takings in wintertime had risen to £88/12/6d per week, comfortably above the original estimate of Mr Mitchell, while in the nine weeks from mid-June to 30 August of the same year they had reached £326 per week. These may have been helped by visitors to the Exhibition of that year taking a sail on the river, since, at a suggestion by Mr Deas, advertisements for the service had been placed in *The Glasgow Herald* from late June, while the *CLUTHAS*, and the harbour ferries, were also mentioned in Elliot's *Popular Guide to the Exhibition*. The summer service was as in 1887, with the exception that one of the service boats now ran to Shieldhall. This development later caused labour problems, since her crew complained that they had to do more work than the other men, but were paid the same. The Trust did not take the hint. However, a rather more human touch was shown by management on 6 April, when employees were allowed to have use of a vessel without charge, to take late-night passengers home after the staff soirée and concert. The passenger figures for 1888 set a pattern for the future; the *CLUTHAS* would always do better in the summer months. With the books balanced, their future was now assured.

The effect of the service on the ferries would seem to have been minimal. The combined revenue from the harbour and Govan ferries increased from £8,827 in 1882-83 to £9,800/15/5d in1884-85 and then declined to £9,252/16/3d in 1885-86 and to £8,895/8/2d in 1886-87. This was well within the figure of the abstraction of c£750 per annum suggested by Mr Mitchell, given that other factors, such as vehicle traffic at Govan, would have influenced these totals.

In October 1889 windows on several members of the fleet were found to have been broken, presumably due to vandalism. The Engineer was asked to repair these as soon as possible and, rather testily, the Ferries Committee minuted that, should this happen again, he was to go ahead with the repairs without waiting for approval.

Occasionally steamers were chartered for river trips and on these they often carried some distinguished passengers. One of these cruises caused some diplomatic problems for the Trust. In May 1886, a *CLUTHA* was chartered to convey a Chinese party, led by the Marquis Tseng, on a cruise around the harbour. The Marquis was the plenipotentiary from the Emperor of China to the Court of Saint James. The British guide for the party, a Mr Smith, afterwards wrote to the Trust to complain that the noise of the engines had prevented an adequate translation being given on board. The problem was referred to the Ferries Committee, who agreed to obtain estimates for a condensing engine. (qv Ch.6). In August 1888 a *CLUTHA* took members of the British Medical Association on a visit to the Fairfield yard and shortly afterwards another provided a harbour cruise for the Institute of Shipbuilders and Engineers.

Pollock's *Guide to Glasgow* in1890 suggested that the vessels had only a basic level of comfort and that, while the sail could be interesting, one should not look for too much among fellow passengers, who were "chiefly of the working classes". The author of the guide went on to criticise the steamers as "not by any means patterns of comfort and cleanliness" and for good measure followed this with a warning about the odour from the river. In the autumn of 1889 there were complaints about steamers missing calls at certain stations and in July 1890 a letter was received from the town clerk of Govan, complaining of overcrowding of the steamers, particularly on a Saturday. In due course he received a soothing reply from the Ferries Committee to the effect that the ships were not really overcrowded, it was simply that most passengers preferred to travel on deck except in wet weather. However, with the growth of traffic, it was clear that a fleet of six boats would soon be insufficient and on 1 December 1890 the Ferries Committee agreed to order two new vessels, authorisation having been received from the Trust. They were to be slightly larger, with a capacity of 300 passengers. Tenders were opened and passed to the Engineer for comment on 30 December and on 6 January 1891 it was announced that the successful tender was the firm of Murray Brothers of Dumbarton.

In November 1890 there was a new problem at Glasgow Bridge landing stage, as water dripping from the railway bridge overhead was damaging the clothing of Clutha passengers. A letter was sent to the Caledonian Railway asking them to attend to the lining of the bridge but this clearly took some time, as a reminder had to be sent two months later. The CR replied that the work was under way and also that engine drivers had been told not to allow locomotives to emit any water when standing on the bridge. As no more was heard of this problem, it would seem that these measures cured the trouble. In the same month, there was correspondence with the Board of Trade about life-saving equipment on both *CLUTHAS* and ferries and as a result of this, the number of lifebuoys on each vessel was increased from six to twelve. The Board considered this to be "very satisfactory". Soon afterwards there was a further problem with sewage at Victoria Bridge, where waste from a slaughterhouse was discharged adjacent to the landing stage and the Trust asked Glasgow Corporation to make alternative arrangements – as no more was heard of this, they presumably did so.

The spring of the following year saw yet another problem at Glasgow Bridge, which was being rebuilt. Two arches of the bridge were closed and it seems that the steamers were either unable to proceed to Victoria Bridge or that the timetable was seriously disrupted, as the Trust sought some kind of compensation from the bridge authority. The latter then took fright and agreed to reopen one of the arches, to allow normal service to be resumed.

03 The Service from 1891 to 1902

By the beginning of 1891 the service had settled down to one of a nine minute frequency, the steamers beginning to run at 7.30am and in winter finishing when the last boat arrived at Victoria Bridge at 8pm. In summer this was changed to 9.10pm and on Saturdays and holidays the steamers continued to sail until 10.30pm. Each boat made ten round trips per day. Calls were made at Glasgow Bridge, Springfield Lane (Kingston Dock), Finnieston (north side, also referred to as Stobcross), Highland Lane, Pointhouse, Water Row (Govan), Meadowside, Sawmill Road, Linthouse (often called Shieldhall) and Whiteinch. To these a landing stage at Plantation Quay was added in June 1897. The total distance was about 3.5 miles (5.6km)

The Ferries Committee agreed on 19 May 1891to implement a 7.5 minute service. This might have put a strain on the existing fleet of eight steamers, but *No. 9* and *No. 10* were in service by 29 June. With these boats in service, it was agreed that the service should be extended to Whiteinch during the Glasgow Fair holidays and until further notice. On 22 February 1892, it was agreed to begin an early morning service between Victoria Bridge and Linthouse and this operated from 1 March. The first boat now ran at 5am, followed by others at 6, (later 6.10), 6.30 and 7.20 (later 7.30), with the regular service beginning at 7.40am. It is not clear how much traffic these early sailings attracted, but in Mr Young's report of 1902, it was shown that only 334 and 385 passengers were carried on 2 and 3 October of that year, out of totals of 4,256 and 4,654 respectively. They continued to run until January 1903. It would seem that the 7.5 minute service proved difficult to maintain and at some point before 1897 a reversion was made to the former frequency of nine minutes, which on 28 October 1897 became eight and a half minutes, from 7.40am to 6.30 pm, with a reduced service thereafter. This level of service still required ten boats, leaving only one spare, as *No.4* had by this time left the fleet. To bring about the acceleration, steamers called at Plantation and Finnieston (north side) on alternate runs and passengers for the other bank crossed free on the passenger ferry. This arrangement did not last for very long, since on 26 January 1898 it was decided to close Plantation stage, with all steamers calling at Finnieston. Possibly competition from the Subway was the inspiration for this improvement. By 1902 the service, excluding the workmen's boats, was operated on an 8.5 minute frequency. In winter the first departure from Victoria Bridge was at 7.20am and the last 6.40pm, with correspondingly later departures from Whiteinch. The summer service ran from April to October and was extended to 7.45pm from Victoria Bridge in April and September, while in the months from May to August the service continued until 8.45pm. All steamers made the full round trip, which took 78 minutes, requiring a speed of about nine knots. Eight vessels were used to run this timetable.

An interesting suggestion was made in May 1891 in a letter from the Trustees of the Cart Navigation, who proposed that a Clutha service should be available to Paisley on Saturday afternoons. The Ferries Committee gave this some consideration but on 29 June replied that they could not provide such a service. The Cart Trustees had a more favourable reply from Captain Buchanan, who ran three of his Clyde steamers from Paisley at the spring holiday of the same year but this did not become a regular service. However, a 7.5 minute Saturday service on the normal Clutha route was inaugurated from 30 June. A later request from the Chamber of Commerce for a boat to convey workmen between Clydebank and Paisley was refused in March 1893.

Traffic was clearly increasing at Whiteinch and in June 1892 it was decided to install a new gangway there for use by boarding passengers.

In October 1892 a blind musician – perhaps the fiddler who played on the Loch Goil steamer *EDINBURGH CASTLE* in summer – applied for permission to play on board the steamers, but this was refused. The employees of the Co-operative Wholesale Society premises in Morrison Street in September 1893 asked for a special sailing in the morning peak, solely for them. The CNT declined to meet this request.

The general pattern of usage was summed up by Mr Young in his report, which was consistent with counts carried out by the Trust staff at various times. In 1898-99 the two city termini were by far the busiest landings, handling 1,018,935 passengers embarking, 36.6% of the total. Victoria Bridge, with 482,928 passengers, was the busier of the two. The next busiest landing was Govan, with 474,768 passengers (17%), followed by Highland Lane with 336,412 (12%). Finnieston (north bank) dealt with 232,609 (8.35%), its heavy traffic being explained by its location quite far from any tram line or Subway station. The least busy stage was Sawmill Road, which handled only 21,537 passengers (0.77%). Other less busy stages were Springfield Lane (91,054), Finnieston south (100,618), Pointhouse (55,322) and Meadowside (85,510). Both Linthouse and Whiteinch were then well-used, with 121,119 and 201,882 passengers respectively. Apparently there were also 30,693 passengers who were counted on board, but it is not clear if these were season ticket holders or passengers who simply managed to board without paying at the turnstile. These all added up to a total of 2,770,459 passengers.

It would seem that there was no heavy morning peak hour traffic on the service, as on 21 October 1902 the first two hours of regular operation, from 7.25 to 9.25am, saw only 10.5% of total traffic, with 447 passengers. Passenger numbers then built up to around the 700 mark (16%) per two hour period, bringing the total for the time between 9.25am and 3.25pm to just under half of the daily total. This would suggest that the service was used by a good deal of optional traffic, which may to some extent have been subject to the weather and likely to decline in winter. The period between 3.25 and 5.25pm was by far the busiest, with all landings showing a considerable increase and the total number of embarking passengers rising to 991 (23% of the daily total). The greatest percentage increase, however, came not at the city termini, where the increase was of the order of 20%, but at Finnieston, almost 30% over the previous two hours, Linthouse (19%) and Highland Lane (43%), while the figure for Sawmill Road remained exactly the same – 6 passengers. These figures were carried over into the first part of the evening, to 6.10pm, suggesting that some people used the steamers for homeward commuting, perhaps as a means of relaxing after a day's work. Again some of this would have been optional traffic and on a cold winter's evening, the brightly lit electric car or the shelter of the Subway would have seemed preferable. The last 90 minutes of service saw numbers drop back to below the level of those handled by the workmen's early morning service. At some landings, such as Meadowside and Highland Lane, evening totals after 6.10pm were down to single figures. The figures quoted above refer to winter weekday totals. Saturday evenings, especially in summer, saw quite a different traffic pattern, but again much of this was leisure traffic. The pattern of usage was consistent with earlier surveys by the CNT staff, although totals had gone down.

There was little publicity for the Clutha service. In 1901, MacDonald's *Guide to the Exhibition and to Glasgow* suggested that "A good view of the harbour and the shipping may be obtained by a penny voyage on one of the Clyde Trust's *CLUTHAS* from the foot of Stockwell Street to Whiteinch, a distance of fully two miles. Unfortunately there is a very disagreeable smell from the river when the tide is low, especially after a spell of dry weather." (as was the case in the summer of that year). That guide also suggested various city tours, to be made generally by car, but no.5 route did include a sail. Having reached Whiteinch by taking the "red car" and duly admired the Fossil Grove and Victoria Park, the visitor was urged to "Proceed down Smith Street and proceed up river on one of the Clyde Trust's *CLUTHAS*. The fare is only 1d but the steamers are not particularly clean and the Clyde smells vilely. Avoid the hours when workers are crowding to or from meals or leaving the yards for the day." It was scarcely an endorsement of the service, but despite MacDonald's warnings, passenger numbers were up in the summer of that year.

The revised service operated from 12 January 1903 was one of a 12 minute frequency between Glasgow Bridge and Meadowside during the day, using four boats, with extension of sailings to Whiteinch at the morning and evening peak hours.

04 Finance

The total cost of setting up the service, as shown in the CNT accounts for 1884-85, was £10,258/14/2d, this being charged to the account of the New Works Committee, not to that of the steamers themselves. There was also a fee of £54/10/- to a consultant, Mr F Edgar of Liverpool. It would appear from Table 2 that the service almost broke even in 1885-86 and made a small profit in the next year. Thereafter revenue climbed steadily until the year 1895-96, after which there was a slight decline until 1900. The decrease in revenue then accelerated and reached a serious level in the year 1902-03, when it was only just over half that of 1899-1900. Working expenses also increased until 1890 then remained fairly constant at £10,000+ per annum for a decade, after which they increased just as revenue began to decline.

With a ten-boat service in 1897, expenditure was as follows:-

Wages	£4,754
Repairs	£2,895
Coal	£2,439
Landing stages	£1,266
Miscellaneous	£1,802

Had the modified service been continued for the year to 30 June 1904, an income of about £3,800 would have been expected, against expenses of over £7,000, assuming no further abstraction of passengers and constant expenses.

Apart from income from passenger fares, the only other sources of revenue were advertising and the weighing machines and "sweetmeat boxes" at the landing places. These are not included in the above figures, but it is unlikely that these brought in much income in any one year. The revenue from advertising for 1897-98 was £230/17/4d and for the following year £154/0/1d.

The capital of the Clutha service was calculated on the amounts paid for the boats and the landing stages and it therefore increased as additional vessels came into the fleet. Initially the total was £13,600 plus £8,071, £21,671 in total. By 1896 these figures had increased to £29,368 and £11,181, in total £40,549. The average over the ten years from 1888 to 1897 was 8.7%. However, there must, for various reasons, be some doubt about the value of these figures, firstly because Mr Aitken reported that the total spent on stages and charged to revenue was £7,164/8/11d, while £11,181/5/7d had been charged to capital and therefore was not shown in the above figures. He went on to claim, in what would seem to have been a piece of creative accounting, that all the stages could be replaced if necessary for a total of less than £4,000, in which case the average return would be one of 10.5%. Nor did this figure take account of the amount of £22,993 for repairs to the steamers, which had been met from the CNT's general revenue account. Had it been included, this sum would in many years have cancelled out any profit made. Moreover, as Mr Young would be quick to point out in his report of 1902, the available figures for the service took no account of depreciation of the steamers or interest on capital and he suggested that it would be necessary to add amounts of £1,576 and £966 (total £2,542) per annum to the above expenses to cover these two items. He could also have mentioned that there was no figure given for a contribution to common Trust services, such as the Dalmuir workshops or the working of the legal department, but these items did not appear in any Trust accounts until some years after the Clutha service had ceased.

Probably as a result of the serious decline in net revenue for the year ending 30 June 1897, a financial statement on the Clutha service, compiled by Collector D Aitken, was presented to the Ferries Committee on 24 September of that year. He gave costs for the existing ten-boat service and also for possible services using eight or six boats. In January 1898 and again in February there was some consideration of selling *CLUTHA No.5* and/or *No.6*, but nothing came of this, though an offer for *No.7*, from an unspecified person, was turned down. Wages, coal and repairs were still the largest items of expenditure, being respectively £3,842, £3,040 and £2,186 for the year 1902-03. The (gas) lighting and maintenance of the landing stages added £588 and repairs to these added a further £722, while general expenses such as advertising cost £77/15/-. The ordinary expenses totalled £11,223/16/3d. This would bring the loss sustained on trading for 1902-03 to £4,385. Several one-off payments had increased the expenses by £843 and it was expected that the usual loss would in future be around £3,500 per annum. Inclusion of these figures would certainly have wiped out most of the profit shown in the above years.

A further statement on the financial position of the *CLUTHAS* was presented to the Ferries Committee on 26 November 1901 and followed by a report in February 1902 (T. CN 3-495) (qv Ch10). These made gloomy reading. The possibility was discussed of running an eight boat service, giving a ten-minute frequency. However, no decision was taken, at either of these meeting and the full summer service began on 18 March.

Given the somewhat erratic accounting, the conclusion has to be that the steamers, although appearing to return a surplus for much of their twenty years of service, were an unprofitable venture for the Clyde Navigation Trust. To put the figures into perspective, it should be mentioned that the total revenue for the Trust for the year 1884-85 was £291,182, for 1899-1900 it was £441,419 and this steadily increased to £553,403 by 1909-10, these figures suggesting a rate of growth of 2.26% and 2.53% per annum respectively. (See Tables 2 & 3)

05 Fares

The basic fare was originally 1d for any length of journey. On 26 August 1886 the Ferries Committee decided that 1d extra should be charged for journeys between the upper harbour and all stages west of Govan. This came into effect on 9 September and was unpopular, since on 18 October complaints were reported about the increase in fares (and also about punctuality, with steamers leaving calling points ahead of schedule). For the week ending 12 October takings were down to £115/4/9d and it was estimated that without the autumn holiday (which seems to have fallen on the Monday of that week) there would have been only £94/16/9d. These figures compared badly with the £138/7/6d for the week ending 7 August. The Ferries Committee resolved the problem by deciding that winter sailings should be on a 15 minute frequency and should go no further than Meadowside, at a fare of 1d. When in April 1887 sailings to and from Whiteinch were revived, nothing more was said about the extra charge. In August 1887 it was decided that six-monthly tickets should be issued for £1 and from 1901 (rather late in the day) there were also quarterly seasons available for 10/6d. These were available on both the *CLUTHAS* and the ferries and the revenue from them was, for accounting purposes, divided in the proportions of 75% to the *CLUTHAS* and 25% to the ferries. Employees of the CNT could obtain seasons at 5/- for six months. This gave about 300 journeys for £1 = 0.8d per journey. On 12 September 1893 the Ferries Committee considered reviving the supplementary 1d fare for sailings from Govan to Whiteinch, but after discussion, it was agreed not to proceed with this proposal and the fare remained at 1d for any distance until the end of the service. In1902 there were 331 holders of season tickets, 183 CNT employees with 5/- seasons and a number of holders of free passes.

In 1891 it was agreed that members of the Boys' Brigade should have free passage when travelling to and from their annual inspection.

There was evidently some fraudulent travel since in July 1886 a ticket inspector was appointed to carry out checks on passengers and in June 1890 a "ticket nipping machine" was bought.

06 Landing Places

Initially landing stages were provided only at Victoria and Glasgow Bridges and Sawmill Road. Ferry stairs were used as calling points at Clyde Street. Finnieston, Kelvinhaugh and Meadowside. Apart from the last-named, *CLUTHAS* called at the stairs on both sides of the river. The existing ferry slip was used at Govan and Partick Wharf served for the Pointhouse call. At Victoria Bridge there was also a coal yard and a berth with workshop facilities, where minor repairs could be carried out on the ships. Major overhauls were undertaken at the Trust's Dalmuir workshops. The stage at Glasgow Bridge was partly under the bridge carrying railway lines into Central Station. It had two gangways leading down from the street, one of which was used for outgoing and one for incoming passengers, since some kind of passenger flow was essential at busy periods.

Landing stages were now used at seven of the ten calling places and were later installed at Linthouse and Whiteinch. At three other places, Pointhouse, Govan West (Meadowside) and (later) Springfield Lane, simple wooden stairs, aligned parallel to the river, were used, though those at Pointhouse were replaced by a floating stage, located between Pointhouse Wharf and the western end of Yorkhill Wharf, after it had been rammed by the laird Line steamer *GARDENIA* on 8 August 1901. This stage, which was the last improvement made to the infrastructure, cost £250/17/10d. The new arrangements outlined above came into operation on 29 December 1884, ending the practice of calling at ferry stairs The exact cost of the works was not recorded, but in the year 1884-85, a total of £10,258/14/2d was charged to the New Works account; deducting the cost of the four ships, this would mean that about £2,000 was spent on the landing stages. There was also a fee of £52/10/- to Mr F Edgar, a consultant. A landing stage was made up of three longitudinal timber beams and rested on two wooden punts, each 32ft 9in (10m) by 15ft (4.55m). The total length was 66ft (20.10m). The gangways were secured to the stages and to an upright on land by safety chains. Plans to construct a landing stage at Clyde Street were discussed by the Ferries Committee on 15 October 1884 but no further action was taken on this point. A landing stage at Shieldhall was discussed in January 1886 and the Engineer duly prepared plans, but in June it was decided that this should be a stair. A stair at Springfield Lane, west of the entrance to Kingston Dock, was constructed and brought into use at a later, unknown date; it was certainly in service by December 1889 and it was damaged by an unknown ship on 22 July of the following year. There must have been some problem with the stage at Victoria Bridge in the winter of 1886/7, since the Engineer and Chairman of the Trust were asked to inspect it, but no details were given, nor did any report follow. The introduction of a vehicular ferry at Finnieston in 1890 required the removal of the Cluthas' landing stage and it was replaced by stairs, designed by the Engineer and located upstream of the new ferry. At some point a stage at Finnieston south side was brought into use; it is referred to in correspondence in 1897. It was not a busy landing, with only 65,533 passengers in 1901-02.

In 1887 an application to allow "Sweetmeat boxes" to be placed on the steamers was referred to the General Manager of the Trust. No further report was made at the time, but machines dispensing sweets were placed on the landing stages in December 1895, the rental for these being 10/- each per annum. Automatic weighing machines were placed on all stages in April 1895, at a rental of £2 per machine per annum. In September 1891 the Ferries Committee agreed to have a coaling ramp and enclosed berth constructed at Victoria Bridge. This proposal had to be authorised by the Works Committee, who agreed to it on 27 October. A Bray's 500 candle power lamp was fitted at Victoria Bridge in 1893 and the 100cp lamp it replaced was in turn installed at Kelvinhaugh.

There were clearly problems with the flow of passengers at peak periods, possibly resulting in some of the accidents mentioned later. In June 1892 the Engineer submitted plans for crowd control at Glasgow Bridge, Highland Lane, Govan and Whiteinch. At the first-named, wooden fencing was to be erected, while the waiting room platform was to be enclosed with fencing at Highland Lane and Govan. These proposals were accepted, but nothing more was heard of about alterations at Whiteinch at this time. However, passenger numbers there continued to grow and in March 1894 Mr Deas was asked to prepare plans for improvements to the facilities at Whiteinch. He did so very quickly and the plans were adopted by the Ferries Committee at its next meeting on 23 April. The main change proposed was the replacement of the stair by a floating stage, which came into service on 27 June. Further plans for this area were discussed in the summer of 1896, when Mr Deas recommended to the meeting of the Committee on 27 August that a new stage should be constructed at Linthouse, 360 yards to the west of the existing one. The next day the Committee paid a visit to Whiteinch and, after making a full inspection of the site, agreed to the proposal, the new landing to be called Sheildhall, although the name of Linthouse continued to be used. They also decided that new stairs should be provided for the ferry and that there should be a waiting room at Whiteinch. These works cost £750. The new stage was opened for service on 8 June 1897.

On 17 October 1894 Mr Deas, following up a suggestion made by the Collector in August, presented to the Ferries Committee a proposal to install new sets of turnstiles at most of the ferry landings (T CN 3-436). As these proved to work well, it was agreed on 4 September 1895 to extend their use to the *CLUTHAS*, with two being placed on each landing stage except for that at Sawmill Road, which was under threat of closure. The total cost was given as £985, with working expenses of £477 per annum. The proposal to close Sawmill Road was rejected at the meeting on 26 November and a single turnstile was duly installed there. All were working by 4 July 1897. Due to the number of passengers using the stage at Glasgow Bridge, it was decided in the following February that those used there should be one size larger. The disruption of the installation of the turnstiles was used to carry out various improvements to the facilities at the stages, for the benefit of both passengers and staff. Victoria and Glasgow Bridge termini saw significant upgrade, with gas fires and lavatory facilities and a new office at the latter being provided, at a cost of £210. Springfield Lane received the same treatment, at a cost of £90. Stobcross was given a gas fire. Extra waiting rooms were built at Highland Lane and Govan. Having been reprieved, and despite its low passenger numbers, Sawmill Road had a new office, a lavatory and a gas supply. Linthouse had the same with the addition of a new gangway and Whiteinch had a new office, a lavatory and a gas fire. Some unidentified work was done for £110 at Pointhouse and Meadowside. In all £1,185 was spent on the works. It is not clear exactly how this was allocated between different sections of the undertaking. Despite all this expenditure, it would seem that the stages still gave a bad impression, since the authors of "*Glasgow in 1901*" refer to the "dingy stages"[1].

On 23 November and 21 December 1896 the Ferries Committee discussed the possibility of calls being made at Plantation Quay and, after a site visit, agreed to go ahead with the proposal on 26 January 1897, having consulted plans submitted by the Engineer. The landing stage, to be located to the east of Mavisbank Quay, was to be suitable for both the Clutha steamers and the ferries. At a cost of £540, the new stage was opened on 8 June. As mentioned earlier, steamers ceased to call at it just eight months later, suggesting that traffic had not lived up to expectations. It was closed on 8 February 1898. Due to the rebuilding of the quay wall, a new stage had to be constructed at Victoria Bridge in 1897.

The works for the new vehicle ferry at Whiteinch had an impact on the service, as on 29 January 1900 the Ferries Committee agreed to move the Whiteinch stage to the foot of James Street, a point to the east of the new ferry recess and more convenient for passengers. Changes of an unspecified nature were also made at this time to the stage at Glasgow Bridge.

1 "James Hamilton Muir" was a pseudonym for three authors. The book was published in 1901 by William Hodges of Glasgow and reprinted by White Cockade Press in 2001.

The Clyde in 1892, showing landing stages/stairs in service at that date, nos. 1-11, and those served at other times (C and P).

Reproduced from OS 1892 6" mapping with the kind permission of the National Map Library of Scotland.

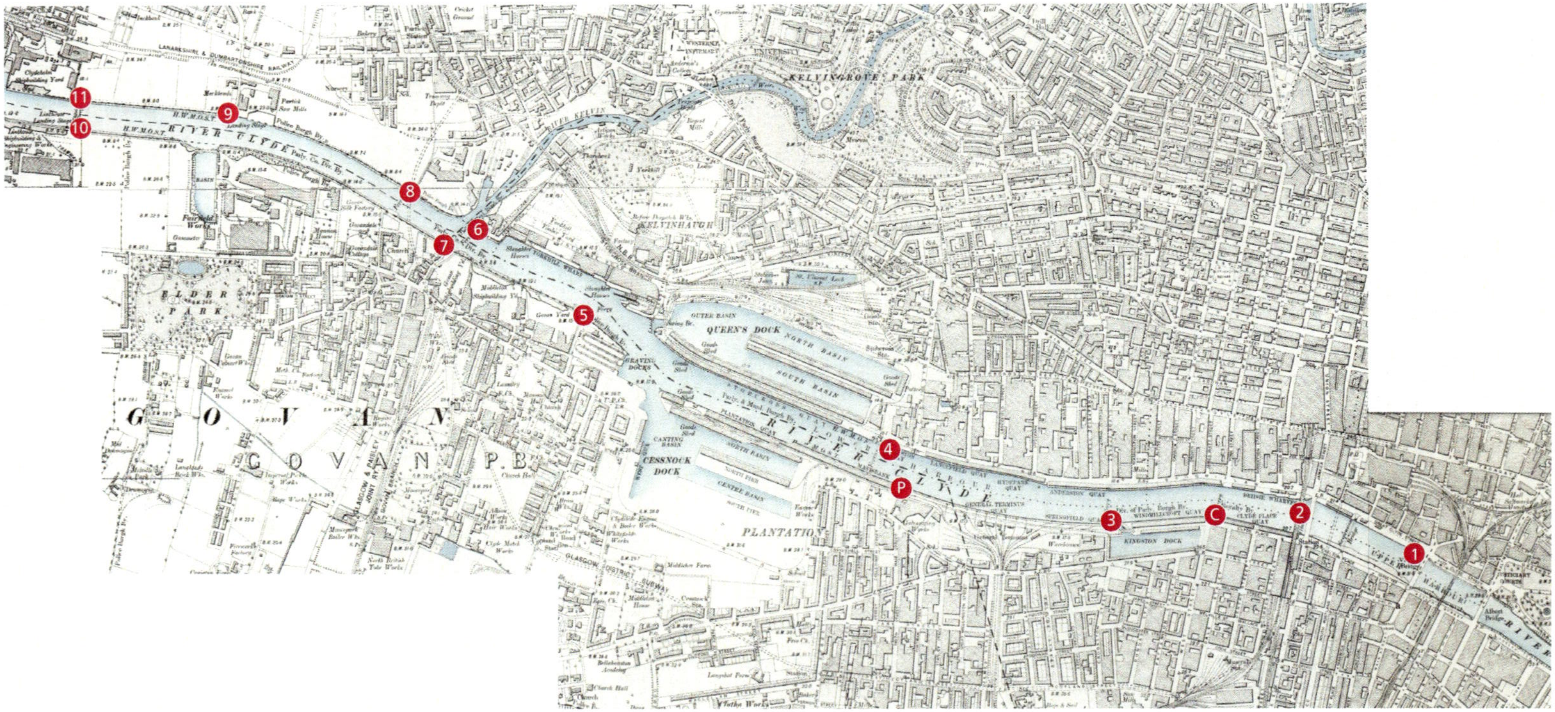

1. Victoria Bridge
2. Glasgow/Jamaica Bridge
3 Springfield Lane
4. Finnieston/Stobcross
5. Highland Lane
6. Pointhouse
7. Water Row/Govan
8. Meadowside
9. Sawmill Road
10. Linthouse
11. Whiteinch

P. Plantation, served only 1897-98
C. Clyde Street, served only in 1884

1. *CLUTHA No.2* in original condition and with a good load of passengers on the lower reaches of the river.

2. A stern view of *No.3*

3. *CLUTHA No.4* when in service, heading upstream past Clyde Street ferry. The steamer lying at the wharf on the south bank is *PRINCESS ALEXANDRA* of Messrs Sloan's Glasgow and Bristol fleet. As she was sold by that firm in1889, this is a fairly early view of a *CLUTHA*.

4. *No.4* after conversion to the CNT yacht. She is seen on the left of this photograph, attending a launch at Clydebank which may well be that of the Cunarder *AQUITANIA* in 1913. The paddle tug in attendance is *FLYING SCOTSMAN* of the Clyde Shipping Company.

5. *CLUTHA No.5*, also heading upstream off the Broomielaw. Another of Sloan's vessels is on the left and some of the Irish steamers of Messrs G and J Burns are on the right.

6. *CLUTHA No.7*, as rebuilt, coming alongside the landing at the north ramp of the Govan horse ferry at Pointhouse, with Partick wharf on the right. A large new ship is on the stocks at the yard of Messrs A and J Inglis, while an equally large vessel lies in the Kelvin.

7. A view of part of the landing stage at Jamaica Bridge, with either *No.7* or *No.8* in original condition with deckhouse. The gangway which led down to the stage can be clearly seen; that for disembarking passengers was on the left. Behind is the outfitter's shop of Messrs Paisley, who specialised in uniforms, for both schoolchildren and for seamen, and a number of horse trams make their way along Jamaica Street.

8. A view of *No.7* in rebuilt condition on the river.

9. With scarcely any passengers, *No.7* pulls away from a landing. The crew member with the bag over his shoulder must have had the job of checking tickets and collecting fares before the introduction of turnstiles.

10. *No.8*, as built, approaching Highland Lane landing stage. A ship of the Anchor Line lies on the right, at Yorkhill.

11. *No.8* At Highland Lane landing stage, where a fair crowd awaits her, with a deal of congestion around the gangway, watched impassively by the master from the steering platform. She is still in original condition and this view clearly shows the deckhouse. It is easy to see how accidents could happen to passengers when boarding or disembarking. This view also gives a good idea of the construction of the landing stages.

12. As rebuilt, *No.8* passes downriver between Govan and Pointhouse. The Govan ferry awaits departure from the north bank and Partick wharf can be seen on the right.

13. Now with a yellow or white funnel with a black top, *No.9* is at the stage of Water Row, Govan. The passengers seem to be quite well-dressed, particularly the gentleman sporting a silk hat.

14. Well laden with a crowd of fairly well-dressed passengers, *CLUTHA No.9* approaches Jamaica Bridge landing under the Caledonian Railway' s original bridge, from which water dripped onto passengers in the early days. An equally dense and well-dressed crowd awaits her. The paddle steamer is *MADGE WIDLFIRE* of the Caledonian Steam Packet Company, working on the service to Kilmun, which the CSP inherited with her from Messrs P and A Campbell.

15. This view of *CLUTHA No.10* at Meadowside shows the layout of the landing at which stairs were used to give access to the ships, as well as the ferry stairs. The vessel appears to be in excellent condition and there are no passengers about, suggesting that this may be a trial run. Behind, a ship takes form in the yard of Messrs D and W Henderson.

16. Water Row landing is, as they might have said, "fair hoaching", as *No.10* calls on her run downriver.

17. *CLUTHA No.11* appears to be in the open sea and this must be a photograph of her on trial. Apart from the master, there are two other men on the steering platform, one in a silk hat. Allowing for the capabilities of contemporary film, it would seem almost certain that she has a red funnel with black top.

18. *No.12* passing the Laird Line steamer *ROSE*, as she makes for Finnieston (north side). (*Author's collection*).

Apart from no.18, all photographs are reproduced by courtesy of the Mitchell Library, Glasgow City Council.

07 Accidents

While the claim made in 1903 by a newspaper that the service had operated for over 19 years without any fatalities was almost technically correct, the little steamers had their share of accidents, perhaps not surprising since they were operating on a river which was overcrowded and at times chaotic, in winter often shrouded in fog. On 18 January 1886 the starboard engine of *No.2* "parted in two" as she was leaving Kelvinhaugh. While this sounds alarming, there were evidently no serious consequences. On the same day, the bow of *No.1* was damaged in a collision with the steamer *GENERAL GORDON*, again without injury to anyone. The first accident which could have been serious occurred between *No.2* and *No.4* off Queen's Dock in fog on 7 December 1886. Another ship, the SS *FURNESSIA* was canting and in avoiding her, the two *CLUTHAS* collided, but again no injuries were recorded. On 12 June 1889, *No.2* collided with Buchanan's Clyde steamer *GUINEVERE* and managed to inflict damage to the value of £105/6/4 and a halfpenny on the larger ship, without being affected herself. At first the Trust declined to pay, but Captain Buchanan persisted with his claim and in January 1890 the matter was settled for a round figure of £80.

The years 1891 and 1892 brought a crop of accidents. On 9 February 1891, *No.3* collided with *MIDGE*, a lighter, and the Clutha master was found at fault by the River Bailie's Court. He was therefore ordered to pay £5 of the damages of £20 which the owner of the lighter claimed. Shortly afterwards, a clerk, T Knox, fell overboard from *No.7*. He was rescued and later argued that the rail had been left open. As this could not be substantiated, his claim was dismissed, but he clearly thought that he had a good case and persisted, until the Trust agreed to settle for £10 on 28 April. In June the gangway on *No.1* was torn off; no details were given but it was in part blamed on the carelessness of the crew. A new folding gangway was to be prepared. On 28 July *No.10* ran into *FERRY No.5* and injured two of its passengers. One was paid £10 damages, but the other did not submit any claim. On the same day *No.1* collided with *No.2*, without injury to anyone, and both masters were fined £1 by the Trust. An action was brought by a passenger, William Short, in October; he had been injured when his legs were caught in the ropes on board a *CLUTHA*. The Trust indicated that the claim would be contested and he settled for £12. Just after that matter, *No.5* was sailed too close to the river bank and the propeller was broken. The master was fined £1. On 9 December the Clyde Shipping Company's tug *FLYING SQUIRREL* was in collision with *No.1* and the Company duly submitted a claim for damages of £92. However, the Ferries Committee were having none of this and rejected the claim on 26 January 1892. The Company pursued the matter and finally in March the Committee passed the problem over to the Convener to settle on the best terms that he could. Agreement was reached on 9 December but the details were not recorded. On 30 January one Lizzie Hutton injured her foot while boarding *No.4* at Victoria Bridge and she was awarded damages of £8 by the Ferries Committee, who clearly accepted blame. No sooner was this dealt with than *No.2* collided with *FERRY No.1* at Highland Lane on 19 April 1892 and in the ensuing chaos, two men, Adam Crenan and James McClymont, tried to jump from the former to the latter and in so doing fell into the river. They claimed damages but the Ferries Committee repudiated all liability. These men were more fortunate than one J Dobbin who fell into the river at Linthouse on 20 August and was drowned. The Committee cautiously agreed to contribute £10 to any fund which might be set up to support his aged parents, but it is not recorded if there ever was any such fund. What could have been a very nasty accident occurred on 21 November 1892 when *No.4* became entangled in a rope stretched across the river from Burns' steamer *DROMEDARY*; fortunately there were no injuries but there were claims for damages and it was agreed to proceed with an action against Messrs Burns. Just two days later, *No.7* collided with the Clyde steamer *BENMORE*, leading to a short suspension for her master. Finally on 23 December *No.5* and *No.7* collided in fog. No one was injured, but the masters were admonished. Possibly in response to this spate of accidents, it was decided that masters should have a bonus of 30/- per quarter if they avoided any accidents. No matter how encouraging this prospect might have been, it was no easy matter to navigate a small ship on a crowded river in the kind of winter weather common in 19th century Glasgow. The problems continued into the new year when *No.10* collided with Laird's *SHAMROCK* on 19 February. The Trust claimed £76 in damages, but in October settled for the £35 offered by the other firm.

Thereafter matters seem to have improved, but there were still some minor incidents. On 11 July 1893 *No.7* was involved in a minor collision with the steamer *KINLOCH* of the Campbeltown Company, no serious damage being sustained by either vessel. The severe weather early in 1895, when the Clyde was frozen over in several places, caused two accidents involving *CLUTHAS*. In the first, on 12 January, *No.2* was carried away from her overnight moorings by the force of the tide, swollen by melted ice, and was found in a sinking condition. She was successfully raised but in March the Clutha Superintendent was reprimanded. In the same week, the owners of SS *LOOKOUT* claimed against the Trust for damage caused to that ship by ice moved by *CLUTHAS*. Liability was declined and no more was heard of the matter.

An accident which clearly alarmed the Ferries Committee occurred at Linthouse stage on 7 April 1896, when a gangway suddenly broke and several passengers were thrown into the water. Fortunately all were rescued and there were no serious injuries, but it could easily have been a different story and the Committee immediately instructed the Trust's Engineer to strengthen all gangways, this work being completed by 30 June. On 9 January 1897 *No.5* was in collision with *Govan No.2* ferry. The verdict was that the masters and crews of both vessels were equally to blame and the master and one deck hand of *No.5* were suspended for two weeks, as were the master, engineer and a deck hand of the ferry. Two more collisions were reported to the Ferries Committee on 27 April 1897. The first involved *No.7* and Burns' steamer *PENGUIN*, while in the second *No.10* had come against SS *MERLIN*. In both cases, it was agreed that each side should bear its own costs, which in the case of the Trust amounted to £120/5/-. On 14 June 1898, *No.9* collided with and sank the steamer *EASDALE* at Springfield Quay, but no details of the accident were given.

There were fewer accidents in the last years of the service, although there was still the occasional contretemps, such as the ramming of *No.7* by the tug *ROVER* on 10 February 1900. The matter was settled for the "modest" sum of £100 and perhaps some blame attached to the Clutha master, who was admonished.

The above account shows that there were indeed accidents, but nonetheless it was an admirable record, given the crowded state of the Clyde at the time, the common occurrence of fog in winter and the fact that, during that season, the ships were operating in the dark for almost half of the working day. The crews must have been skilled men indeed.

08 The Steamers

CLUTHA No.1, No.2, No.3 and *No.4*

These four ships were built by T B Seath and Company of Rutherglen and engined by J G Kincaid and Company of Greenock. They were described as originally having open bows, which meant that there was an opening in the bulwarks, to allow passengers to board and disembark by the stairs at ferry landings. As this practice proved to be unsuccessful, they were rebuilt about 1890 with the deck being carried up to the bow. In November 1885 it was reported that oil fuel was being tried on *No.2* and that *No.4* was to be fitted with a new, upright boiler. In March of the following year, the boilers of *No.2* and *No.3* were being repaired while the experiments with *No.2* continued, now using Baird's fuel, no details of which were given. The trials of oil fuel were discontinued in February 1886, but the use of compound fuel (again no details given) on *No.1* continued until October of that year, when the Ferries Committee ruled that there should be no further experiments with this. In December 1886 an offer was received for a surface-condensing engine to be fitted to one of the ferries of this class. The matter was referred to the Engineer. On 19 January it was agreed to accept this offer, which seems to have come from Kincaid and Company, as a test. *No.4* was discussed at the meeting of the Ferries Committee on 1 July 1887 and it was agreed to re-engine her, as the crankshaft and condenser were both defective. The contract did not go to Kincaid but was given to a firm named Walker, Henderson and Company and the steamer was ready for inspection by 9 September. However, problems must have continued since she did not then resume service and in December Walker, Henderson reported that they had made a loss on the order. It was, however, agreed to pay them, retaining a small balance during the trials of the new machinery. These were obviously not totally satisfactory, since in February 1888 it was mentioned that there was bulging of the combustion chamber. By April *No.4* was working satisfactorily and the balance of the account was to be paid. It would seem that this did not happen, since the matter went to arbitration and in December 1888 the contractors were awarded £23, rather than the £93 which they had claimed. In July 1889 the Works Committee authorised the fitting of a new boiler to *No.3*. *No.4* was reboilered at Dalmuir in June 1892. After successful trials of Rayner's feed-water heaters on *No.1* and *No.3* early in 1889, it was agreed that these should be fitted to all other *CLUTHAS* and also to all ferries. In July 1890 approval was given to fit new "upright" boilers to *No.1, No.2* and *No.3* but only the latter two received these, one being fitted at Dalmuir and one by Messrs Marriott and Graham. The number of problems with the machinery on what were almost-new steamers was clearly considerable and the Trust members must have been disappointed with the quality of the workmanship.

In December 1895 there was consideration of selling five of the first six *CLUTHAS* for £1,250 each, *No.4* being initially excepted. After the alterations to her machinery, *No.4* was unable to keep to the timetable and was now said to be "unfit for service"; she was therefore added to the above list, to be sold for £1,000. However, on 18 February 1896 the Ferries Committee agreed to pass her over to the Works Committee for conversion to a launch. The work was carried out at Dalmuir, where she was slightly rebuilt and renamed *COMET*. In this capacity she served the Trust until 1947. In the event the proposed sale did not go ahead and it is difficult to see how the service could have been maintained at its usual frequency without these vessels. In August 1898 the question of selling *No.1, No.2* and *No.3* was again discussed, again without result. The three steamers were finally offered for sale in December 1902, but *No.1* was in the event retained by the Trust as a launch. *No.2* went to Denny of Dumbarton, though it is not clear what function she performed for them. *No.3* was sold to a firm of stevedores at Grangemouth on the Forth and changed hands several times until broken up in 1907.

Length 72ft (21.9m), width 13ft (4m), draught 5ft 4in (1.61m) 235 passengers. Cost £2,000 each

CLUTHA No.5 and *No.6*

These were the additional boats ordered in 1884. They too came from T B Seath's yard and again had machinery supplied by Kincaid. They were much larger than the first four and had a passenger capacity of 350. They soon came to the notice of the Fire Brigade, who in November 1885 asked permission to use them for fire-fighting duties. This was declined on the rather lame excuse that the boats did not have steam up at night. Further to the problems of noise which had spoiled the cruise of the distinguished visitors from China (qv Ch 2), the Ferries Committee on 18 October 1886 received four tenders for condensing engines. As *No.5* and *No.6* were then laid up for the winter, they seemed to be likely candidates for any experiment, but in the event they were not used for this trial. These two steamers also had a nasty habit of showering the deck with hot cinders and in 1886 damages were paid to a child who had had his neck burned on board *No.5.* It was mentioned that *No.6* was "just as bad". Despite this failing, the latter was chosen to convey members of the joint committee, formed from the Trust's Harbour and Ferries Committees, down river to Renfrew on 2 November 1889, to inspect the first high-level vehicular ferry boat, then under construction at Simons' yard. New boilers for these two vessels were approved in May 1895. As mentioned above, it was planned in December 1895 to sell these two ships, along with *No.1*, *No. 2* and *No. 3*, but as the only offer received for them was of £1,000 per vessel, they were withdrawn from the sale list and put back into service. In January 1898 an offer was received for either of the two ships and the Convener was instructed to negotiate with the potential purchaser, but nothing came of this approach. In December 1900 it was decided to fit compound engines to the two steamers, to give a saving of £260 per boat per annum. *No.6* was also given a new boiler and in all the alterations cost £1,580. She resumed service on 23 January 1902 and it was reported that the new engines had resulted in a saving in coal of 22cwt (1.22 tonnes) per day, but it is not clear if they were ever fitted to *No.5*.

No.5 was sold to owners in London and was used for some years on the Thames. Her sister went to Wilson of Bo'ness, by whom she was used for cruising on the upper reaches of the Firth of Forth until 1913. Strangely, she was still known as *CLUTHA No.4* and her name was not changed to suit her new employment. She was by far the most suitable excursion steamer in his fleet, which otherwise consisted of antiquated paddle tugs, and was often the vessel chosen for charters. However, in1913, following the loss of *TITANIC*, Mr Wilson decided that he could not afford to equip his fleet with the new life-saving equipment now required by the Board of Trade and she was abruptly withdrawn in mid-season. She saw some kind of war service on the Forth but did not return to pleasure cruising on it afterwards, being sold to a Mr MacGillivray in Macduff. She was broken up in 1926.

Length 102ft (31.35m), width 17ft (5.24m), depth 8ft 6inches (2.6m), 350 passengers. Cost £2,500 each

CLUTHA No.7 and *No.8*

These two boats were authorised in the autumn of 1889 and on 29 October the tender of Murray Brothers of Dumbarton was accepted, with the proviso that Mr Nairn (manager of the Dalmuir workshops) should be able to inspect the work at any time. Their engines were manufactured by M Paul and Company, also of Dumbarton. They entered service in July 1890. Originally these vessels did not have an after cabin, but instead a deckhouse, extending the entire width of the ship, was fitted on the after deck. The builders had also offered to make them flush-decked, but the Ferries Committee declined the proposal, although the Engineer was asked to obtain estimates from the Dalmuir workshops for carrying out this work. In the event nothing more was heard of it and it would seem the deckhouses did not prove satisfactory, since on 29 January 1895 the Ferries Committee decided that these should be removed and a cabin fitted below. The cost of the alteration was £132 per vessel. The work was carried out at the Dalmuir workshops by February 1896 and the steamers could now carry about 60 additional passengers.

Both steamers went to the Tyne in 1904, having been sold to Messrs R W Hawthorn, Leslie and Company, to convey workmen on a ferry service on that river, essentially similar to their work on the Clyde. They were renamed *HEBBURN* and *WALLSEND* respectively. The former was lost by sinking after a collision in 1940 and her sister was withdrawn in 1949.

Length 76ft 5 inches (23.32m), width 16ft, (4.88m) draught 5ft (1.52m), 315 passengers, later 375. Cost £2,665 each.

CLUTHA No.9 and *No.10*

In November 1890 the Ferries Committee gave some thought to the running of a ten-minute service, which would have been impossible with the existing fleet of eight steamers. Authority was duly obtained from the Trust to order two additional vessels and Murray Brothers were successful in the tendering process, begun on 13 December 1890. They were both in service by 29 June 1891. Slightly larger than their immediate predecessors, they both had compound engines, by M Paul and Company, the first use of compounding in the fleet. Both were sold to the Admiralty in May 1905 and their subsequent history is not known.

Length 87ft (26.8m), width 17ft 1inch (5.25m), draught 6ft (1.8m). 360 passengers. Cost £2,830 each.

CLUTHA No.11 and *No.12*

On 4 February 1896 the Ferries Committee discussed the possibility of ordering two new boats, on the model of *No. 9*, but larger. It was agreed to go ahead with this proposal, but within weeks it was decided that they should actually be slightly smaller than their immediate predecessors. Tenders were opened on 24 March and that by Russell and Co, Port Glasgow, at £2,665 per vessel, was accepted. Compound engines were supplied by Muir and Houston of Port Glasgow. They were taken over by the end of August of the same year and by January 1897 were reported to be giving satisfactory service. These boats were built to Lloyd's full seagoing classification, but the upkeep of this was ultimately too much for the Ferries Committee and on 28 August 1899 it was resolved not to continue to maintain them to this standard. After serving as the last *CLUTHA* in service on 30 November 1903, *No.11* was sold to the Corporation of Bangor, North Wales and after war service, went to Middlesbrough, where she was renamed *LADY MAGDALEN*. By 1936 she was running on a ferry service in Milford Haven. Her later history is not known. On the cessation of service, *No.12* went to the north of Ireland for service on Lough Neagh, renamed *LOUGH NEAGH QUEEN*. In 1908 she returned to Scotland to sail on Loch Leven, as *LOCH LEVEN QUEEN* and in1911 passed to David MacBrayne

Ltd. She was then transferred to maintain the mail service on Loch Ness in the following year and was renamed *LOCHNESS* to suit. When it ended in 1928, she was sold for scrapping at Inverness in1929.

Length 87ft (26.8m), width 17ft (5m). draught 6ft (1.8m), 330 passengers. Cost £2,550 each. (It is not clear why the ships cost less than the initial quotation)

The layout of all the steamers was standardised. The upper deck ran for almost the entire length of the vessel and the main deck below it was divided into five compartments. At the bow there was a small compartment for stores, followed by the fore saloon, 15ft (4.57m) in length and extending the entire width of the hull and having wooden seating along each side. The third compartment contained the engines and boiler. The after cabin was 25ft (7.62m) long and had a toilet in one corner, with seating as in the fore cabin. It was a non-smoking area and so presumably used more by ladies. The cabins would have been somewhat claustrophobic and according to *The Engineer*, were only used when the weather was inclement. They were lighted by rectangular windows, except on *No.7* and *No.8*, which had portholes in the fore saloon. The general condition of the steamers may also have left something to be desired, since an additional cleaner was appointed in January 1889. In view of Pollock's comments (qv Ch2), he had clearly not made much impression on the problem within a year. Given that many passengers would have been in working clothes, on their way to or from heavy and often dirty (and dangerous) work, it is perhaps not surprising that it was difficult to keep the steamers clean. On 25 February 1901 it was decided that a trial of steam heating should be made on one steamer, but there is no record of the outcome of this, nor of which vessel was so fitted. The experiment cost £30/3/7d.

All steamers were twin-screw and the propellers were used to steer them into and away from landing stages. In view of the frequent stops, particular attention was paid to the valve gear, for which simplicity and strength were the main attributes. Hinged funnels were fitted. The engines were kept running all the time that the vessel was in service. Until *No.9* and *No.10* arrived, all steamers had simple-expansion engines and compound engines were fitted retrospectively to *No.6* and (possibly) *No.5*. Despite the lack of success with earlier experiments with oil fuel, the Ferries Committee discussed on 24 July 1893, the possible adaptation of a steamer to burn oil fuel, following trials on the Caledonian steamer *CALEDONIA*. No further action was taken.

It is clear that there was a perennial problem with smoke from the steamers and the Ferries Committee made several attempts in the early 1890s to find some means of reducing the emissions. The "Don" smoke consumer was tried on *No.5* and *No.6* in the winter of 1890/1, but was found to be unsuccessful. In April 1892 Cube's briquettes were tried, along with William Auld's smoke prevention apparatus and, on *No.3*, the Whittle Steam Injector Company's smoke consumer. The Committee persisted with the first two of these, but refused permission for a continued trial of the last. They then turned to the Sennett smoke consumer, which at first seemed to show some promise but soon proved to be so unsatisfactory that permission to continue with it was refused, even when the Sennett company offered to guarantee the results. The Committee minutes rather drily recorded that there was no reason to think that better results could be guaranteed and with that the experiments came to an end.

The livery of the steamers varied from time to time and definite information is not given anywhere. On 22 December 1884 it was agreed that the livery should be that of the harbour ferries, which would imply a black funnel and india-red hull. However, it appears from photographs that the original livery was a cream or white funnel and a black hull, with white lining. Later it seems that steamers had a red funnel with black top. On 16 April 1897, it was agreed that all vessels should be painted as *No.11*, but it is not clear what the livery actually was.

Despite the early problems, the *CLUTHAS* seem generally to have been well-built little ships and *Nos.1,4,6,7,8, 11* and *12* were all still in service in 1923. The last two to sail were *No.4* (until 1947, at the age of 63) and *No.8*, which was not withdrawn until 1949, at the age of 59.

09 Personnel and Passengers

The first Convener of the Ferries Committee during the time of the Cluthas was James Lockhart Mitchell a native of Glasgow, who had been involved in the sugar trade with the West Indies, later becoming a partner in the firm of Edmiston and Mitchell of 33, Renfield Street. He was first elected to the Trust in 1880, as a representative of the ratepayers, and became Convener of the Ferries Committee in November 1883, a post which he held until his death on 6 June 1893. He was a member of the Free Church and interested in yachting. As mentioned earlier, he was largely responsible for bringing the Clutha service into operation and, according to the biography in "*Men you Know*" would have liked to have seen a five minute service. When Mr Mitchell died (it would seem unexpectedly) he was replaced by Bailie Robin Guthrie, of whom little is known. He remained in post only until November 1895, when he was replaced by T C Guthrie.

T C Guthrie was a native of Dumfriesshire and came to Glasgow about 1870 to enter the business world. Ultimately he became a shipowner himself, founding a line of sailing ships named after villages in his native county. Like Mr Mitchell he was a member of the Free Church, but his hobby was not a nautical pursuit but bowling. *The Bailie* noted with some disapproval that he was unmarried and hoped that he would soon find a wife to share his fine property in Bellahouston. Mr Guthrie was replaced as Convener in November 1899 by William Bilsland, but he remained a member of the Committee until after the demise of the service.

Sir William Renny Watson (1838-1900) was an engineer who specialised in the production of sugar-refining machinery. He became a member of the Trust in 1880, as a representative of the Corporation of Glasgow and became Convener of the New Works Committee, in which capacity he became closely involved in the Clutha service, particularly in matters relating to the landing stages. However his main achievement was the construction of the graving dock at Govan. He was also a member of the board of the Glasgow and South Western Railway and became its Chairman in 1890.

The Engineer to the Trust for most of the time that the *CLUTHAS* ran was James Deas, who was in post from 1869 until his death in 1899. After an engineering apprenticeship, he joined the Glasgow and South Western Railway, then moved to the Edinburgh and Glasgow Railway as Assistant

Engineer. He was perhaps disappointed not to have been appointed Chief Engineer of the North British Railway when the two companies merged in 1865 and in 1869 he moved to the Trust, with which he remained for the rest of his career. He was an able engineer and oversaw the construction of Queen's and Prince's Dock, as well as doing a fair amount of consultancy work, which at one point brought him a reprimand and fine from the Trust. Ultimately, however, his salary was £1,500 per annum, a very high figure for the time when £200 per annum was considered a good wage. It was strange that someone of his calibre went so badly wrong with the question of the use of the ferry stairs by the *CLUTHAS*.

(Information on these gentlemen is taken from the series "*Men you Know*" which appeared in the magazine *The Bailie.*)

Alexander MacPhean was appointed Superintendent at a date before 1892 and clearly gave much more satisfaction than his predecessor, since in October of that year it was agreed to increase his wages from 45/- per week to 50/-. It is not known how long he remained in post and it would seem that in later days the most senior officer was Collector W Alston.

Each vessel had a crew of four – captain, engineer and two deckhands, one of whom was a young lad, usually referred to as the rope boy. One who started his career in that way finally retired as master of the Govan vehicular ferry on her last run in1966.

During all the time that the service operated, inflation was virtually zero in Britain, apart from normal seasonal variations. In November 1886 the crews petitioned for an increase in wages but this was refused. The men returned to the matter in October 1887 in a letter in which they pointed out that they worked an eleven hour day but were paid only for ten hours and that they had no meal breaks. The matter was referred to the General Manager and Collector to "arrange something" which they presumably did, since industrial peace reigned for the next five years. Along with the ferrymen, the crews returned again to the fray in March 1892, this time adding longer holidays and a uniform to their list. All that they got from this was a kind of uniform, as they were issued with serge jackets and caps; this would have meant that they no longer had to provide their own coats. Later in that year, several men on both ferries and *CLUTHAS* were suspended, no details of their offences being given and in September a master, William Francis, was dismissed "for reasons stated by the Collector". As dismissal for faults in navigation was rare, his must have been a serious offence, perhaps of a financial nature. However, in April 1894 all ferrymen, engineers and turnstilemen were granted an increase in holidays from 10 to 12 days, this being holidays with pay. For the time, this was a generous allowance, and on reflection the Trust must have decided that it was too generous, since the amount of holidays with pay was reduced from two weeks to one week on 25 April 1897 – this applied to both the harbour ferries and the *CLUTHAS*. (T.CN3.474). A full uniform for ferry and Clutha crews was provided in 1901.

In January 1895 it was agreed that the turnstilemen should have between 3/10d and 4/2d per day and that displaced ferrymen should be offered employment at the turnstiles at 3/6d per day. Thereafter all vacancies at the turnstiles were to be filled by youths at 10/- per week. By 1902, only girls were employed in this work.

In 1902 the establishment, with daily wages paid, was as follows:-

1 Inspector	7/6d
1 Collector	5/-
8 Masters	6/8d
8 deck hands	4/2d
8 engineers	5/-
8 rope boys	2/6d to 3/2d
2 cleaners	3/6d per night
2 coal men	4/4d per night
1landing stage cleaner	3/4d
18 turnstile girls	1/4d to 2/-
1 Sunday watchman	6/3d for the day

Apart from the last-named, all worked a ten hour day. The number of turnstile attendants was greater than the number of stages to allow three hours relief to be given to all during the course of the day.

Occasionally an engineer was hired to clean the engine rooms.

No additional payments were made for overtime.

The Trust did not have a superannuation scheme until 1908 and it would seem that crew members went on working as long as they were able. At the discretion of the Ferries Committee, grants were made to those who retired and it seems that the members did give some thought to these and were not ungenerous. The amounts were usually in the region of 5/- to 7/6d per week. There was no variation in the amounts awarded to crews on the ferries and the *CLUTHAS*. In May 1903 a Clutha engineer, William Gallagher, aged 73 and with 29 years service, was awarded a weekly pension of 7/6d, a considerable reduction on his wages of 30/.

Of the passengers, nothing is known. The only mention of the steamers in literature is in Neil Munro's "Erchie" and then it is only brief. Erchie and his wife Jinnet embark on a *CLUTHA* for Whiteinch, but Erchie gets off at Govan by mistake, leaving Jinnet to make her own way home. But the little ships did find their way into one Glasgow street song, a verse of which ran:-

I hiv a friend who kent a man that bet a friend a fiver
That he would jump Jamaica Bridge like Tommy Burns the diver.
The folk aboot the Broomielaw kicked up an awfy shindy
For he dived right doon the funnel o' *CLUTHA number twinty.*

(Chorus)
Hey boys, d'ye think I'm fly?
It's the only way I've got.

Tommy Burns was a man who made his living by doing stunt dives from a great height at the Crystal Palace, at resorts such as New Brighton and, without permission, from the Forth Bridge. Unfortunately a dive from a height of over 150ft (45.72m) at Rhyl in the early 1890s went badly wrong – he landed on his back in a choppy sea and was killed. There were apparently many verses to the song, all separated by the chorus given above. One recounted the problems of a Mrs MacGee, who "tried to whustle and broke her bustle" – this reference would suggest that the song dated from the 1870s.

This information is taken from correspondence in *The Glasgow Herald* in 1964.

10 Competition and the End of the Clutha Service

When the Clutha service began, competition was limited. On the north bank of the Clyde, the horse trams of the Glasgow Tramway and Omnibus Company ran a through service as far as Whiteinch, but the Argyle Street/Dumbarton Road corridor lies quite far inland and at that time, there was a dense population living near the river, for whom the steamer service would be more convenient. On the south side the tramways were nearer the river, but the Glasgow trams ran only as far as Parkhouse Toll (now Paisley Road Toll), where passengers for Govan and Linthouse had to change to the steam trams of the Vale of Clyde Tramways Company. Apart from the inconvenience of the break of journey, this meant that the through fare was 3d to Govan and 3.5d beyond, though passengers could save 1d by riding on the upper deck. As this was not covered, exposure to smoke and smuts added to the discomfort and these trams therefore offered little competition to the steamers. The Vale of Clyde Company had had its best year in 1882, when it carried 3,385,914 passengers and paid a dividend of 6%. Thereafter a decline set in and the effects of the *CLUTHAS* were soon recorded in falling passenger totals and shrinking receipts. The Company, which had responded by increasing the frequency of the cars, constantly complained about what they saw as unfair competition from the Clyde Navigation Trust, who could afford to run a service at a loss (and did not take into account the start-up costs of the new service when fixing fares). It seems that on the other side of the river, the Glasgow Tramway and Omnibus Company experienced similar trends on the Whiteinch service, but of course it was a much larger concern and that service was only a small part of its network.

The position remained unchanged until 1893, in which year the Govan Burgh Commissioners (councillors) evicted the Vale of Clyde Company on termination of its lease and instead passed this over to the Glasgow Tramway and Omnibus Company. Very soon after this take-over, a through service of horse trams from the city was begun, the trams having to run via Paisley Road West and Lorne Street to avoid complaints from Glasgow Corporation. The latter took over the lease on 11 November 1896 and later began a service via Govan Road. There was no mass transfer of passengers from the steamers to the trams and the through fare was still 2d, but there must have been some who deserted the boats for the new, improved cars. This change of operator was very soon followed by the opening of the Subway on a permanent basis on 21 January 1897, the fare from Govan to Glasgow being at first 2d but this was reduced to one penny ha'penny in October 1901. Again there was no great loss of passengers and the main CNT activity to be affected was the local ferries, but a three-minute headway, enclosed (if unattractive) stations and an 18 minute journey time from Govan to the centre of Glasgow must have attracted some away from the steamers. This, together with a steep increase in working expenses, reduced the surplus on the operation of the service from £4,523 in 1895-96 to £596 in 1896-97 and the return on capital from 12.47% to 1.32%. On the north bank of the Clyde, the opening, in stages, of the Lanarkshire and Dumbartonshire Railway (a subsidiary of the Caledonian Railway) in 1896 may also have taken some traffic from the steamers, since it offered a through service from the east end of the city and Central (low level) to Whiteinch and beyond, with intermediate stations at Anderston, Stobcross and two in Partick. Curiously the Trust had supported the plans for this line when they were first put to Parliament.

However, it was to be the electric tram which brought about the end of the service within a very short space of time. While the Trust members bothered themselves about the condolences to be sent to Kaiser Wilhelm II on the death of his mother, the Empress Frederick, the trams were spreading all over the city. They reached Partick on 28 April 1901 and on 12 May the service was extended to Whiteinch. On the south bank, the overhead wires reached Govan on 10 August 1901, via Paisley Road West and Lorne Street and a more direct service via Govan Road began on 24 March 1902. In June 1902 the penny stages on the tramways were extended to cover a distance of over two miles. The combined effect of the electrification and the reduction of fares was immediate and disastrous and a statement of the financial position of the Clutha service was presented to the Ferries Committee on 26 November 1901, with a report by Mr Stewart, Traffic Superintendent, following on 18 February of the next year (T. CN 3-495). The takings for the six months from 1 July to 31 December had been almost identical in 1900 and 1901 (£5,737 and £5,747), but the figure for 1901 concealed an increase in July and August, perhaps due to traffic generated by visitors to the Exhibition and a drastic decrease of over 20% in the last months of the year. Mr Stewart was pessimistic. He considered introducing a halfpenny fare for two or three stages, but did not favour this, as there would have to be an increase in passenger numbers of 500,000 to show any gain in revenue and he doubted if this would happen. The alternative was to introduce discount tickets, as used by 38% of passengers on the ferries. He thought that this might attract traffic, but there would still have to be an increase of 334,720 passengers if the scheme were to break even.

In the event, neither of these suggestions was adopted by the Ferries Committee. At the first of these meetings, it was agreed to run a service of eight steamers on a nine/ten minute service and to review the position at the end of the financial year. In1902, as recorded in Mr Young's report, the situation became even more catastrophic, being now exacerbated by a decline in summer traffic.

The matter had been considered at the meeting of 26 August 1902 and in view of the continuing and increasing loss, it was agreed to discontinue the service on 31 December. The only dissenting voice was that of the Convener, Mr Bilsland, who suggested continuing for a further year. However, as there seemed to be no possibility of increasing revenue, the question was carried and the proposal then went to the Management Committee, who on 2 September supported the decision. An offer by an unidentified private firm to take over the service was not entertained. However, on 28 October the latter Committee received a deputation from a special committee of Glasgow Corporation, consisting of Councillors Campbell, Forsyth and Miller and John Young, General Manager of the Tramways Department. The representatives explained that the Corporation wished first to confer with the councils of Govan and Partick, whom they would be meeting later in the day, and in view of this, the decision was put on hold for the time being.

Glasgow Corporation had meanwhile become alarmed at the possible loss of the steamers and on 2 October 1902, on a motion of Councillor Campbell, set up the special committee mentioned above to look into the question and to consider what steps might be taken, should it be considered that the convenience of a large proportion of the citizens would be affected by the closure of the service. On 17 October the committee held its second meeting at which it was agreed that a delegation should meet members of the Clyde Navigation Trust and also that Mr Young, should be asked to prepare a report suggesting improvements which might be made to the service and its financial position. Unlike present-day consultants, Mr Young, with the co-operation of the General Manager of the Trust, prepared his report with commendable speed and it was submitted to the meeting of the committee on 27 October, but as the meeting with the Trust had been arranged for the next day, it was agreed not to consider it until the next meeting on 17 November. It made depressing reading. By the year 1901-02, the number using the two city termini had gone down to 840,226 passengers but this was still over 36% of all passengers. The third busiest landing was still Govan, with 326,838 passengers embarking, 14.1%, of the total while Highland Lane, with 275,236 (11.8%) was still in fourth place. Sawmill Road had meanwhile increased not only its total, to 29,836 but also its percentage share to 12.9%. The pattern of decline was not quite universal and Finnieston (north bank) had also increased its total to 241,215 passengers. On the other hand, Springfield Lane had seen a decrease in numbers of 21.75% and Finnieston (south) one of 35%. Some stages saw very few passengers; Sawmill Road had only 46 (1%) passengers embarking on the entire day of 21 October 1902 and Finnieston (south side) only 119 (2.7%). Many steamers must have called at these last two stages without embarking or disembarking any passengers. The total number of passengers in July, August and September 1901 had been 879,296, while in 1902 these months saw only 620,365, a loss of 29.45% of traffic. The total from 1 to 20 October 1902 was only 93,874 and even if an additional 50% is added to cover the notional period to the end of the month, this figure would only reach about 140,000. There had always been a decline in wintertime, but not on this scale. The number embarking at the city termini went down from 88,377 in October 1901 to 29,882 from 1 to 20 October 1902, indicating a probable loss of over 50% over the whole month. The pattern was repeated at every other landing, with only slight variations. Only Meadowside seemed to be immune from the disaster.

As detailed above, the meeting with the Committee of Management took place on 28 October and the only concrete result of it was that the Trust agreed not to take any further steps to withdraw the boats until the matter had been considered by the full Corporation. At the meeting with the representatives of the councils of Govan and Partick, who had indicated that they would like the service to continue, the idea of some kind of joint subsidy to keep the service going was suggested by the Committee members but received without enthusiasm, the delegations from the two burghs stating firmly that they had been given no authority to consider any such proposal. A "general conversation" followed and the burgh representatives hinted that, in view of the improvements recently made to the tramway and railway services in their areas, the value of the river service was now limited.

With no help forthcoming from the neighbouring authorities, the Committee considered Mr Young's report at its next meeting, held on 17 November. The steamers were well maintained and smartly operated and there was no scope for economies. There were no periods in the day when the service could be reduced. Most of the passengers appeared to be travelling on general business and had no connexion with the harbour. The rather small minority who did were generally travelling on season tickets or free passes. It went without saying that few took advantage of the service for pleasure sailing "in the general condition of the river".

There were workmen who used the steamers to reach the shipyards morning and evening and, to a certain extent, at "breakfast and dinner times". (It was, until the 1960s, quite common for people in all kinds of employment in Glasgow to go home for the mid-day meal and, in the case of shipyard employees, it was evidently also common to start at an early hour then have a meal break about

9am.) These people might be inconvenienced, Mr Young said, but the entrances to the shipyards were usually in streets away from the river and the Subway and railway services could accommodate them, while the tram service for workmen was "always increased with the demand". He expected that the Trust would also improve the ferry services if the *CLUTHAS* were withdrawn, though they had given no commitment about this and in the event did not do so. Only those who would have to use a ferry then travel a distance up or down the river bank would really have a problem. In any case, he added, the main flow of workmen's traffic was in the lower reaches of the river and these people were not Glasgow ratepayers. All the other passengers could reasonably be served by other forms of transport. There was in fact already some local agitation for a line down Finnieston Street, though Mr Young may not have known of this. That line finally opened on 4 June 1904 and was consistently underused and unprofitable all through its short life. It was the first tram line in the city to close, on 4 May 1925.

With perhaps a trace of a crocodile tear in his eye, Mr Young remarked that everyone would be sorry to see the service go, as it had been a feature of the river and closely identified with the city. However, it was clear that the Trust did not want to continue with a loss of £3,500 per annum and in the circumstances, it was very difficult to find any justification for the Corporation stepping in to relieve it of this large annual loss for the benefit of a comparatively small number of people.

Having digested this report, the committee met on the following day and agreed to recommend that the Corporation should not proceed any further in the matter. They then discharged themselves. The Corporation accepted the recommendation.

On 1 December the Committee of Management of the Trust noted that the Corporation did not wish to proceed further on the question. At the same meeting, however, it was agreed not to withdraw the service but to institute a six-month trial with four boats. The Ferries Committee on 16 December accepted this decision and announced that the reduced service would begin on 12 January 1903, with the four steamers providing a twelve minute headway between Glasgow Bridge and Meadowside during the day, with some sailings being extended to Whiteinch during the morning and evening peak hours. *No.1, No.2,* and *No.3* were then offered for sale. While the new service would certainly save on working expenses, it was optimistic to imagine that a reduced frequency would help to combat tramway competition, when there was virtually "always a car in sight" in Govan Road and Dumbarton Road. The new timetable duly came into operation on 12 January 1903 and nothing further was said about it until the financial results for the period from that date to 25 April were made available. For this period of just under 15 weeks, the takings were

£946/1/8d, about £63 per week. There was a slight improvement in the takings for the 23 weeks to 20 June, with a total of £1,620/16/9d, about £70 per week, a drastic decline from the figure of about £244 per week in 1897-98. This was by no means enough to save the *CLUTHAS* and the Committee of Management proposed that the service should be withdrawn as from 30 November, the decision being confirmed by the Ferries Committee on 18 August. By that date, *No.5* and *No.6* had already been sold. There was no further debate. Revenue from 1 July to 30 November was £1,595/17/-, equivalent to £72 per week, but costs were £2,936/7/7d, about £133 per week.

(See Table 2 for details of income, expenditure and net revenue)

11 The Last Run

Monday 30 November was a cold, dreich winter's day, with by evening a clammy mist and drizzling rain. The Trust had perhaps been expecting a large crowd to turn out – perhaps on the scale of that which, in even worse weather, would bid the trams farewell in 1962 – and a considerable number of policemen were in evidence at the Glasgow Bridge landing stage when *CLUTHA No.11* drew in to take the last departure at about 6pm. In the event, the constabulary had nothing to do. Only 32 passengers were on board when the vessel left the stage. There were four old gentlemen, who were evidently enthusiasts, four ladies, two of whom had regularly for the past seven years travelled on the last boat from Linthouse, six clerks from the Trust's head office, who came along "for the lark" and who enlivened the proceedings by some "harmless horseplay", and two gentlemen of the press. These joined 16 others who had boarded on the up run, afraid that they might not have been able to board in the city because of the crowd. One of these, a Mr Blair of Govan, claimed to have held a season ticket since the start of the service[1]. Mr Grieve and Inspector Alston represented the Trust and the Captain was William Smellie[2], "the oldest in the service". The other crew members were James Thomson, engineer, John MacMillan, collector and Alfred Hunter, rope boy. A few more passengers joined on the way downriver – a family at Govan, a very stout gentleman at Meadowside and a very slim gentleman at Linthouse. The voyage back turned into something of a triumphal procession, *No.11* being saluted by the Clyde Shipping Company's SS *PORTLAND*, a hopper, a collier, the Meadowside ferry, the Govan vehicular ferry, her counterpart at Finnieston, the *CLAN FORBES* coming out of Prince's Dock and the outward-bound Dublin steamer *DUKE OF FIFE*. To each of these, *No.11* answered bravely and so came to Springfield Lane, where the last-ever passenger to board a *CLUTHA*, a lad of about 15, came down the gangway, to the cheers of those on board. He said that he had come "for fun". Victoria Bridge was reached at 7.17pm and the passengers disembarked, the pressmen being the last to leave. One newspaper account also reported that several passengers took a turn at steering the ship on the last run and that a collection had been made for the crew but had not been very large – given the number of passengers, this was hardly surprising.

1 Season tickets were first made available in 1887.
2 McQueen gives the name as Sinclair.

Epitaph: *Who killed the Cluthas?*

Who killed the Clutha?
I, said the car, as I'm popular:
I killed the Clutha.

Who saw him die?
I, said the Clyde, on my turbid tide,
I saw him die.

Who'll dig his grave?
I, said John Young, to life he has clung;
I'll dig his grave.

Who'll be the chief mourner?
I, said the Trust, with heartfelt disgust:
I'll be the chief mourner.

Who'll toll the bell?
I, said the car, with a clang and a jar,
I'll toll the bell.

Evening Citizen, 1 December 1903.

("Car" in this case of course means "tram" – a usage common in the city until the end of the trams in 1962.)

No.2, No.3, No.7, No.8 and *No.12* were sold just before the service ended and an offer was to be accepted for *No.11. No.9* was then on hire to an unidentified firm in Greenock and was to be sold on the termination of this. *No.1* was being used at Dalmuir works and was not to be sold. *No. 9* and *No.10* were not sold until March 1905, when they fetched £1,700. The stages at Victoria Bridge, Stobcross, Highland Lane and Sawmill Road were removed and nine pairs of turnstiles had already been sold when the service ended.

A curious postscript was put to the Ferries Committee by a company named the Clyde Boat Company Ltd, who proposed to run a service from the city to Dalmuir, with 16 boats and were looking for some moral if not financial support. The Committee declined to be involved in any way and it was not until 1938 that any short-distance passenger boats again ran on the Clyde. In that year the Caledonian Steam Packet Company placed the motor vessels *ASHTON* and *LEVEN* on a sightseeing service from Bridge Wharf to Clydebank and back, with no intermediate calls, at a fare of 1/-. The service ran again in 1939 but was discontinued on the outbreak of war. No service operated in the post-war years until the Garden Festival of 1988 brought a waterbus service to the Clyde, with vessels modelled on those on the canals in Amsterdam. The service did not last very long, but in recent years the firm of Clyde Marine has run a regular service, from Easter to October, between Glasgow and Braehead, with calls at the Riverside Museum, giving passengers a taste of what it must have been like to sail on a Clutha.

Table 1: Passenger numbers

1884-85	1,113,328
1890-91	2,177,974
1893-94	Over 3 million
1894-95	3,253,438
1895-96	3,172,834
1896-97	3,555,117
1897-98	3,495,610
1898-99	2,782,609
1899-1900	2,765,383
1900-01	2,630,867
1901-02	2,316,726
1903 to 30 June	464,528

Table 2: Total revenue, working expenses and net revenue from 1884-85 to 30 June 1903. These figures were calculated from 1 July to 30 June of the next year.

	Revenue	Working Expenses	Net
1884-85	£4,638/17/6d	£5,855/19/8d	-£1,217
1885-86	£5,299/17/10d	£5,349/11/4d	-£49
1886-87	£5,613/15/2d	£4,794/2/6d	£819
1887-88	£6,731/15/4d	£5,292/1/3d	£1,439
1888-89	£8,088/7/4d	£5,254/19/8d	£2,803
1889-90	£9,157/14/6d	£6,192/2/9d	£2,965
1890-91	£11,021/16/11d	£9,400/1/4d	£1,621
1891-92	£12,753/11/9d	£10,946/15/4d	£1,427
1892-93	£13,712/9/-	£10,800/1/5d	£2,912
1893-94	£14,211/16/-	£10,443/10/6d	£3,768
1894-95	£13,361/12/7d	£10,800/8/1.5d	£2,519
1895-96	£14,967/3/3d [1]	£10,443/16/6d	£4,523
1896-97	£13,842/7/9d [2,3]	£13,246/7/9d	£596
1897-98	£12,121/8/3d	£10,338/14/2d	£1,439
1898-99	£12,064/6/11d	£10,862/8/8d	£1,382
1899-1900	£12,002/12/4d	£10,738/14/2d	£1,684
1900-01	£11,387/2/11d	£12,696/4/4d	-£1,309
1901-02	£10,124/3/3d	£12,057/1/11d	-£1,933
1902-03	£6,168/7/5d	£7,437/17/11d	-£1,251

1 Through service of Glasgow Corporation horse trams to Govan.

2 Opening of Lanarkshire and Dumbartonshire Railway line on north bank, in stages between May and October 1896, with passenger service from 1 October. Stations on the route of the *CLUTHAS* were at Glasgow Cross, Glasgow Central, Anderston, Stobcross, Partick (two stations, Central and West) and Whiteinch Riverside.

3 Subway opened on a permanent basis in January 1897. Halfpenny fare introduced between Govan and Partick Cross in June.

The figures given above are taken from CNT accounts and do not in every case correspond with those given in the table used by Mr Young, but the differences are not significant.

Table 3: Return on capital. (T. CN 3-445)

1887-88	6.80%
1888-89	13.30%
1889-90	14.02%
1890-91	5.29%
1891-92	4.22%
1892-93	8.63%
1893-94	11.15%
1894-95	7.46%
1895-96	12.47%
1896-97	1.32%

Bibliography

Apart from the undermentioned sources, all material in this book has been drawn from the records of the Clyde Navigation Trust. The minute books used were in the series T. CN 1 13-18.

Glasgow Tram Services. David L Thomson. The Scottish Tramway and Transport Society and Venture Publications Ltd. Glasgow 2009.

Minutes of Glasgow Corporation Tramways Committee. 1901-1903.

The Ferry System at Glasgow Harbour, in *Engineering*, 24 December 1897.

Clyde Harbour Passenger Steamers. Report to the Special Committee of Glasgow Corporation by John Young, General Manager, Glasgow Corporation Tramways, Glasgow, 25 October 1902.

Clyde River Steamers of the last fifty years. Andrew McQueen. Gowans and Gray Ltd, London and Glasgow, 1923.

Clyde River and Other Steamers. C L D Duckworth and G E Langmuir. Brown, Son and Ferguson, Glasgow, 4th edition, 1990

Steamers of the Forth. Ian Brodie. David and Charles. Newton Abbot, 1976

Circles under the Clyde. John Wright, Capital Transport, London, 1996

Accounts of the ending of the service and the final run are taken from the following:

Glasgow *Evening Times*. 30 November 1903

Glasgow *Evening Citizen*. 1 December 1903

The Glasgow Herald. 1 December 1903